Chicago's First Family

Chicago's First Family

By Paris Davis

So You Can Write Publications, LLC
PO Box 80736
Milwaukee, WI 53208
www.sycwp.com

Publishing date: 8/25/2022
ISBN-13: 978-1-7376084-7-9

Cover design by: www.sycwp.com
Printed in the United States of America

(Note: "The majority of quotations gathered by the author have been frequently in print and/or movie and television, as well as publicly accessible on the Internet; considered public domain. Where possible, the author and publisher have made their best efforts to credit any available sources for them. In the cases where it was uncertain where they first appeared, the information was cited as "unknown" or "anonymous." The information in this book is intended to uplift and inspire all who read it, or who have it read to them. The information quoted was kept as it was found and/or heard by the author, who makes no guarantee that the information one-hundred percent accurate, just that the author intended for it to be beneficial to all who reads it, or has it read to them."

SO YOU CAN WRITE
PUBLICATIONS®

<u>Dedication</u>

I want to dedicate this book to my heart, my brother and sister, Aisha & Demar. I love you both to death.

- Paris Davis -

Chapter (1)

"**M**J, come here," my mother said in a weak voice from her hospital bed.

"Yes baby," I responded looking at her.

My mother was looking very different; she'd lost her hair, voice, weight, skin tone, and swag. Moms been fighting cancer for the last two years and she had finally lost the battle. I was thinking before she called my name again and it broke me from my thoughts.

"MJ, I need to talk to you while I still can. Now baby, I don't need you to respond just yet, I just want you to please listen because this is already hard for me," she said with tears in her eyes. "MJ, your father was a good man…"

"If he was so good then, where is he now?" I said looking at her.

"MJ, please let me talk…" she paused and reached under her pillow and handed me a picture.

It was a picture of her and someone I knew that had to be my father because we looked like twins.

"MJ, he never knew about you because I never told him I was pregnant. I took some money from him and left once I found out I was pregnant with you because I didn't want you to grow up in that life. But somehow, you've found yourself on that side of the fence anyway," mom said while coughing.

Blood was coming out as she put a towel up to her mouth. Once she finished coughing she continued talking.

"MJ, find your father and tell him I'm sorry. He's in Chicago somewhere, and please don't be mad at me, please. Your father's name is Jamel, but everybody calls him Melly, that's why I call you MJ for Melly Junior, after your father. Not because of basketball. MJ, I don't have much time to live and you're out here in this world all alone, so please find your father," mom said looking at me, but I didn't respond. "MJ, promise me you'll find him?" my mother asked with tears in her eyes.

I couldn't believe moms knew where my pops was the whole time we've been living in New York and we've been here for three years. Before that, we've lived in Texas, Wisconsin, Iowa and about five other places. I was never able to have true friends because we never stayed anywhere long enough and I never was able to get a true education.

Everywhere we lived I was robbing or selling drugs to help moms pay rent or I was always fighting because I was the new person; or I was just different. I was always thinking I was alone, now I found out my father didn't leave us, we left him.

Looking at the picture I seen that we were both tall, both of our complexion is the shade of peanut butter, we both have light brown eyes, a fat nose and long arms. I wonder, how is he? Did the streets sharpen his mind the way it sharpened mine? Is it hard for him to trust people the same way it is for me?

"MJ, promise me?" I heard my mother say waking me up out of my day dream. She started coughing again and blood came out on the towel again.

"Mom, I promise I'll find him, and what's his name?" I asked looking at his picture unable to meet her eyes.

"Jamel Jones, the same as yours."

All this time I thought my name was MJ because I liked to play basketball. I stood up and kissed moms on the forehead, then walked toward the door.

"Mom, I'll be back I have to make a run real quick." I didn't have to make a run I just needed some air.

I left the room not knowing if I would ever hear my mother's voice again. One hour after leaving, she died. I seen she had got her last skeletons out of her closet before she left us.

* * *

I left out of the hospital and inhaled the cool May air as I jumped on the train heading home to our two-bedroom apartment in the projects in New York. Walking through the building's stairs and hallways I seen Bear and Tom-Tom standing in the vestibule, selling crack.

"What's up MJ, are you hustling today?" Bear asked pulling out a roll of money.

"Naw bro, I'm chilling today because I have a lot on my mind, my mom is sick," I told Bear walking pass him.

Bear was a big nigga, he was 6 foot 6 and was black as tar, with long dreads. Bear ran the building I was living in and I've been working for him for about two-in-a-half years, off and on.

Once I made it in the house I went to my room and grabbed my weed, then rolled two blunts and grabbed my half pint of Patron off the dresser. I sat on the bed and blazed the blunt while my mind drifted back to pops…how was I going to find him? Where was I going to look? Plus, I could tell moms was getting worse because she was coughing up blood now. I was so deep in thought that it took me a minute to hear my phone ringing, when I grabbed my phone and looked at the time, two hours had passed since I left the hospital.

"Hello?" I answered not recognizing the number.

"Is this Jamel Jones?" Some lady asked sounding sad.

"Yes."

"Well, Debra Smith has passed, could you please come up here and view the body and also sign the paperwork? You were her next of kin," the lady said before hanging up the phone.

I knew mom was going to pass, but not this soon. I left the house and got on the train headed back to the hospital. Once I made it there, mom's body was already downstairs in the freezer, I looked at my mother and she had a smile on her face. For the first time in years she looked happy. I signed the papers for her and they told me I had a week to come and get her body. I left the hospital thinking, I was glad mom had gone because that meant she didn't have to suffer anymore, but it hurt that my best friend was gone.

Mom passed at 43 years of age alone. Now here I was 21 and, in this world, alone. Once I made it home, I got on the internet and found a funeral home that said they would do all the arrangements. The burial, casket, dress and make-up for $8,300. I didn't know you had to pay so much when someone passed. I looked in my stash and I only had $5,000, so I called the funeral home and told them I had $5,000 now and would have the other $3,300 at the burial. They agreed.

So, I jumped on the bus to take them the money and informed them which hospital mom was in. The funeral director said they'd handle everything from there. I left the funeral home on my way to the building knowing that I would have one-week to get the remaining balance for the funeral cost - $3,300.

Once I made it to the building I seen Bear and I pulled him to the side and explained to him what was going on. Bear said he was going to let me work for the next week to make the money I needed to bury moms. Over the next week I tried to make and save as much money as possible, but the more I stayed up and worked, the more I smoked and t drank. I wasn't the only person working like Bear said, so by the end of the week I had saved $4,000 and most of that was going toward mom's burial.

I buried mom on June 1st, and the only people that showed up beside myself was the preacher and two other people to throw dirt on mom's casket. When they started lowering her body into the ground it started raining really hard like the world felt my pain. After they put mom in her grave I sat on the ground and cried like a baby. I said to myself, "these are the last tears that will ever drop from my eyes again…"

*   *   *

The next couple of days was stressful for me. First, they cut the lights off, then they put another five-day notice on the door. I only had $300 and Bear didn't want to let me work anymore. Tom-Tom and his crew were working from sun up to sun down. I was standing down stairs in the hallway when Bear walked in the building and Tom-Tom handed Bear the take for the day.

"Bear, let me work!" I asked watching all the customers come through the door.

"Man MJ, you have to holla at Tom-Tom because he has the floor."

"Yeah, nigga, I already told you that," Tom-Tom said smiling and walking away leaving me and Bear alone in the stairwell.

"Well, Bear, you already know my moms just passed so do you want to buy some of her jewelry? I need the money," I said walking toward my house.

"Let me see what she got," Bear replied following me, I could feel him smiling behind my back.

Once we walked through the door of my house Bear closed the door behind him, I told him to lock the door over my shoulder. When Bear turned around from locking the door, I hit him with everything I had and he crumbled to the floor like a rag doll unconscious. I grabbed the sheets off my bed and tied his hands and feet up really good. Then I put a sock in his mouth and tied a sheet around his head. I began to grab all our pictures from around the house, and the book bag mom kept all her important paper work in. I searched Bear taking a Glock-19 off him, $6900 and his car keys.

When I started walking out the door, Bear started moving and trying to free his hands from the sheets that I had around them. I put the book bag over my back and slapped Bear across the head on my way out the door and said,

"You should have let me work!"

I went down the stairs and out the back of the building. Then I jumped in a cab. I told the cab driver to take me to the train station. When we arrived at the train station I got out the cab and went inside to purchase a ticket to Chicago. The train was leaving in one hour, so I decided to go over to the food court and get some McDonalds while I drifted off in my thoughts. How was I supposed to find someone in a place like Chicago as big as it was? The only clue moms told me was that pops was from the Westside so I guess that's where I should start looking, but what would I say if I found him? Was pops even still alive or was he a crack head like most nigga's fathers were, or did he want to see me? The way mom was talking, pops was getting money so I should hit up the clubs and ask all the dope boys. I came out of my day dream when I heard, "Boarding the train to Chicago in slot 4."

I asked the first train attendant I saw where was slot 4 and he pointed over his shoulder to the right. I boarded the train and sat down letting my thoughts return to moms. I was out here by myself, and hopefully, I could find pops before I ran out of money. I had $7,000 and I wasn't trying to start back robbing in a city like Chicago.

Chapter (2)

When I woke up we were thirty minutes outside of Chicago, I got up and walked down the aisle to go to the bathroom. On my way back to my seat I saw a pretty chick sitting down with an empty seat next to her, so I sat next to her and started talking to her.

"Excuse me miss lady, but are you from Chicago?"

"Yeah, why?"

"It's just that I need some help with something, I wanted to know if you were looking for somebody and didn't know your way around, or didn't know where they could be found, what would you do?" I asked her.

"Boy, I don't know," she said popping her neck like a hood rat.

"Well, could you at least tell me where the clubs are that all the dope boys go to?" I asked while getting a better look at her.

Everything about her was phony… fake nails, fake hair, fake eye lashes, fake Gucci purse. I started smiling and took out a real fifty-dollar bill and handed it to her. She instantly put it in her purse and took out some paper and a pen. She wrote down five names putting a star by two of them. All of them were located downtown around the place where the train was stopping. The ones with the stars be popping on Fridays she said. She got up and walked off holding her purse tight as hell.

When the train stopped, I got off and found ten cabs out front waiting so I jumped in one and told the driver to take me to the cheapest hotel that was still in the downtown area. The cab driver took me to Division and Clark street, to the Mark Twain hotel. On the way to the hotel I asked the driver where were the hot spots downtown and he said 'Red Lights' was a hot club. I just so happened to be one of the clubs that was on the list. We pulled up to the hotel and when I got out I couldn't believe how fucked up and ran down the hotel was.

I walked into the hotel and asked how much was a hotel room for a week, and the men at the front desk said three hundred. So, I handed him four hundred and told him to give me his best room. He gave me a room on the first floor that was freshly painted with new sheets. I placed my bookbag down in the room and came back out to asked him where a rental car place was located. He told me there was an Enterprise right around the corner. I walked out and went to Enterprise to rent a car, and thirty minutes later I was pulling out on the Chicago streets.

I drove down Division toward the west side, lost. I stopped at a store called City Sports, on Division and Milwaukee. I bought two Lacrosse linen shorts sets, one white and one white with baby blue - with a pair of all white Bally's, along with a Lacrosse hat. While I was in the store I heard some girl on the phone talking about how her nigga was locked up, and how she was going to hit the club this weekend. So, I instantly went next to her and acted like I was looking for something to wear. Once she hung up her phone I asked her,

"Sweetie, where are they smoking at?"

"On Homen or Ridgeway," she said looking me up and down. She was a black ugly bitch, but her body was bad as hell.

"I'm not from around here and I don't know where that is."

"Look, I'll show you where it is, but you got to smoke with me."

"Okay, that's cool, but are you driving?" I asked walking to the counter to pay for my things.

"Naw, what about you?" She asked walking behind me with a Gucci jogging suit that I knew was too tight. There was no way all that ass was going to fit in there.

As we walked out the store I asked her what her name was and she said Princess. I couldn't help but to laugh to myself. I told her my name was MJ and we walked over to the car. The whole time I kept saying to myself this ugly motherfucker is thick as hell. I had rented a Buick so I popped the trunk and put my bags inside and she put her things in the back seat.

"Do you have your driver license?" I asked her.

"Yeah, why? Do you want me to drive?" Princess replied excitedly.

"Yeah, and where is your nigga because I don't want to get nobody in trouble."

"Boy, I can't get in trouble, and anyway he locked up, but what you trying to buy a dub?" She asked returning to him smoking with her.

"Naw, I want an ounce of some kill, and take me to the liquor store; you drinking with me?" I asked turning on the radio and letting my seat back.

She took me through the city and we talked. I found out she was twenty-one with no kids and lived with her sister. We went to the liquor store and grabbed a fifth of Remy, and two packs of honey backwoods. Then she pulled up to a house on Homen, and told me to give her one hundred and fifty dollars. She jumped out the car and went into the

13

house. Cars kept pulling up, and ten minutes later she came out of the house and got in the car passing me the weed. I could smell that it was some kill.

"I'm sorry it took so long, but it was some niggas in there that didn't want to let me out. They were trying to fuck," she said starting up the car and pulled off. "Where to now?" she asked while I was breaking the weed down for the wood.

"It doesn't matter, just hit the city and tell me who is who and who doing what and where, and show me where the hot clubs are," I said rolling the blunt.

"Okay, well, where we just left from are the Dirty Block Nigga's," she said driving.

She took me all around the city. While she drove, I rolled up the weed and poured the drinks. We rolled around until one thirty am and people were riding around like it was two o'clock in day time. I could tell Princess was getting tipsy because her eyes were getting glossy. So, I told her to pull over somewhere safe, and somewhere that the police are not going to fuck with us. She pulled over on some street called Madison, a park called The Circle. When we pulled in, there were around a hundred cars parked there. We found a parking space and I looked over to her while I was breaking down another wood.

"Chunky pour me some Remy."

"Who are you calling Chunky?"

"I am not calling you Princess anymore, I'm calling you chunky, that's my name for you, is that a problem?" I asked grabbing my drink from her while passing her the wood to light up.

"I guess not," she said, grabbing the lighter off of my lap and lighting the wood.

I told her let's step out of the car and I leaned up against the driver side door, and she put her ass on my dick as she passed me the wood from behind her head. I sat my drink on the hood of the car and took my hand slipping down her jogging pants and started rubbing on her pussy. She instantly opened her legs and put her head back up against my chest. I put two fingers inside that pussy and it was tight and wet, she started grabbing my leg pushing her pussy against my hand. I took my hand out of her jogging pants and smelled my fingers, her pussy smelled fresh.

"Chunky, where can we grab something to eat at this time?" I asked getting back into the driver seat and starting the car while she walked around to the other side of the car and got in.

"Pull out and turn left, then stop when you see the sign 'Taste Buds' about six blocks down," she said grabbing the weed. I saw the sign and pulled over.

"What do you like?" She asked passing the wood.

"It doesn't matter," I said going into my pocket to grab the money.

But before I could grab the money she had jumped out of the car and ran across the street to the restaurant. I sat in the car thinking how was I going to play this? First, I knew I needed this bitch to show me around town, but if I hadn't never learned nothing from mom is that, don't no bitch want no tender dick as nigga. So, when she got back in the car I asked her where did she live, and she said by the store where we brought the clothes from. I asked her how do we get back there, because I was staying down the street. She directed me to Division and told me the store was on that block, just keep straight down until I see the store.

Chunky had dozed off and when she came back to I was pulling across Ashland, a block from the store.

"Where do you stay?" I asked slowing down across the street from the store.

"I stay in that building right there, but I want to go with you," she said looking down.

I pulled off and went to the gas station down the street, she didn't want anything so I got out and brought a box of condoms, two bottles of water, and put thirty dollars in the gas tank. I pumped the gas and shot down the street to the room. We got out of the car and went to the room with Chunky carrying our food. Once we got in the room she threw everything on the bed and ran to the bathroom saying she had to pee. I took her phone and put it on the nightstand next to me, then I put my gun under the pillow on the side of the bed I was sleeping on.

I grabbed some food out of the bag and when she came out Chunky was naked, and I must say her body was flawless. She was so thick it made her look pretty, but when I looked at her she was different. The whole time she had been wearing a wig, Chunky had some long ass hair, and she had been wearing some long ass fake eyelashes, she also had washed that make-up off her face. Chucky wasn't pretty but she was okay. She sat on the bed and grabbed her food, I took off my shorts and shirt, but kept my boxers and tank top on; and we talked while we ate.

I found out that Chunky stayed with her sister and her sister's nigga who kept trying to fuck on the low. She had been fucking with some nigga name Tony for five months, but he been locked up for three weeks. We finished our food and I lit the half of wood I had put out in the car. Chunky asked where her phone was at and I said I had it, I tried to pass her the weed instead, but she said NO and grabbed my boxers.

She pulled my boxers down and grabbed my dick and then started deep throating it while she was rubbing my balls. I was trying to hold off as long as possible, but ten minutes later she swallowed my nut and asked me if I had rubber. I told her no and she looked like she couldn't believe it. I started rubbing her pussy and it was dripping wet, so I stopped playing with that pussy, as bad as I wanted to fuck her, I told her we'll get one in the morning. I cut the TV off and laid down. For the next ten minutes I felt the bed shaking, then she rolled over putting her ass on me and went to sleep.

Chapter (3)

I woke up to Chunky sucking my dick, once I busted a nut she said there was a Walgreens across the street, so I told her to jump in the shower and I would be right back. I went across the street and grabbed a pack of tank tops, some boxers, soap, deodorant, and toothbrush. Once I came back Chunky was on the bed playing with her pussy. I told her we had to bounce and I jumped in the shower, got dressed and we left.

I pulled up to Chunky's parking lot and told her to go put some clothes on because she was going with me. I stayed in the car and told her to hurry up. Ten minutes later, she came down in a one-piece spandex skirt that came right above her knees. It was yellow and white with some yellow and white air max with no sock. Her seat was still let back from last night so when she got in I could see she didn't have any panties on. We went to some breakfast joint called Bus Bond on Kedzie, right off Jackson street. It wasn't nothing but dope boys in there eating and I told Chunky I was trying to find my pops.

An old black man around sixty with a pot belly and short hair brought our food, I decided to ask him if he knew somebody named Melly. He told me to let him finish his orders and he'll be back, when he walked off Chunky was saying that we had to go to this bar where all the old timers be on Pulaski and Lake. It was where all the old-time hustlers be. By this time, we had finished eating and the old man came walking back to our table.

"Why are you looking for him?" He asked looking me in my eyes. Now, I didn't want to tell anybody he was my pops because I didn't know what he was up to. So, I said,

"My mom made me promise to tell him something on her deathbed." He must have seen the tears in my eyes when I spoke about my mom because he said,

"Yeah, Melly used to come in here all the time, but I haven't seen him in almost ten years. Check down the street on Jackson and Kedzie at that barber shop. He used to always get his haircut there," and he walked away, then turned back around and said, "and young blood, anybody that really knows Melly already knows he's your pops because you look like his twin. So, you might as well keep it up front," then he walked away smiling.

After he left, me and Chunky walked to the car and she drove down the street to the barber shop. The old man who was in there did a double take once I walked through the door. I asked him how many people he had in line and he said two, I said okay and sat down. Chunky went to the other side of the shop and asked the lady how long would it take to perm and blow dry her hair. Then Chunky came back to me and asked if she had an hour, I said yeah, then I grabbed my phone out of my pocket because it was ringing. I knew it was a New York number, but I didn't know who it was.

"Yeah, what up?" I said into the phone, but before I could finish Bear was screaming through the phone.

"Bitch ass nigga Imma kill you once I catch you…"

But I had already hung up and put the phone on vibrate as my mind went back to my pops. How was I going to find him? I came out of my day dream when a booster came up to me asking if I wanted to buy a Gucci jogging suit with a pair of Gucci shoes. I asked how much and he said one-thousand dollars. I checked the size and then pulled out five-hundred-dollar bills and told him to take it or leave it because that was all I had. He took the money and left.

I jumped up because I was next in the chair, and when I walked passed I heard two niggas talking about how they were about to buy the Gucci shit, then one of them started mean mugging me. So, I kept walking to the chair and smiled.

"What's your name young blood?" The old man asked as soon as I sat down

"MJ," I said watching the two niggas leave looking my way.

As it turned out, Old School did know my pops. He thought I was him, but he said he hadn't seen pops in around five-years, but told me to leave my number and he would make some calls and call me if anything came up. Just as I was getting up Chunky was walking toward me, I paid Old School and grabbed the bag with the Gucci clothes were in. Then I grabbed my gun from out the back of my jogging pants and put the bag in front of me so I can hide the gun in the same hand. I hugged Chunky around the neck and told her let's go.

We had parked half a block down from the parking lot, and just like I thought, the niggas got out of a car and started following us. So, half way to the car I stopped and turned around with one hand wrapped in the bag holding the gun and the other arm still around Chunky's neck.

Once we turn around, one of the niggas had a gun out smiling and he spoke first.

"A funny man, give me the bag and all your money," he said upping his gun.

Chunky instantly put both of her arm's in the air, so I started passing him the bag and told Chunky to put her arms down because the police were driving pass. When I said that, he put the gun on the side of his leg and turned around looking in the direction I was looking in, but before he could turn back around toward me I shot through the bag and hit him in the shoulder on the side he was holding the gun. He instantly dropped the gun and the other guy that was with him took off running. I told Chunky to pick up his gun and we started speed walking to the car.

"Chunky, don't drive fast, just drive regularly and go to the hotel," I said watching Chunky drive looking scared as hell.

*   *   *

It took us twenty minutes to make it to the hotel. I gave Chunky the key and told her to take the gun and clothes to the room. I took the car back around the corner to Enterprise and traded the Buick for a 2018 Chrysler Town and Country minivan that was all black with light tint. I went in the hotel and knocked on the door and Chucky answered looking scared. When I walked into the room she was rolling a blunt.

"MJ, what happened back there?" Chunky asked not looking up from rolling the blunt.

"Nothing, just some niggas playing around, but any ways, what's up you feel like hitting the club tonight?" I asked throwing the lighter on the bed next to her.

"Well, it's early as hell. What are we going to do until the club tonight?"

"Let's go check that old timer's bar out you were talking about a little later, but I'm going to relax now." I said reaching for the blunt.

We both had nodded off and when we woke up, it was eight o'clock. I grabbed my phone and ordered a pizza and jumped in the shower, Chunky was laying on her back with her leg up watching TV and smoking the last of the blunt.

I walked in with a towel around my waist and dropped it once I reached the edge of the bed, Chunky raised up and grabbed my dick. She started deep throating me trying to look me in the eyes. While she

19

was sucking my dick, she put her hand between her legs and started playing with her pussy. I tried to hold my nut, but watching her play with her pussy, and her moaning I couldn't hold it and I started nutting everywhere.

I then told her to turn around and put her ass in the air, she got on her knees and slid her hand between her legs and started playing with her pearl tongue. I went and got a rubber from out of the bag that was on the floor and put it on. My dick was still on limp from nutting so I just started slapping my dick against her pussy while she was playing with her pearl tongue. Every time I slapped her pussy with my dick her pussy juices jumped all over my stomach.

Chunky started saying please MJ fuck me, and by now my dick was rock hard. I start rubbing my dick up and down her pussy and she started cumming saying, "…please fuck me." I put the head of my dick inside and Chunky started shaking trying to push her ass back against my dick. I pushed my dick all the way in and when I pulled out it was cum everywhere on the rubber. Chunky started rubbing her pearl tongue faster and I started speeding up. I long dicked her for thirty-minutes before I felt myself about to nut again.

Chunky's pussy was soaking wet, and she started cumming, reaching back trying to push my legs. I couldn't hold it and nutted, then fell on the bed breathing hard as hell. I looked at Chucky, she was still shaking.

"Why you do me like that?" Chunky asked.

"Like what?" I said looking at her since she had taken all that fake shit off.

She looked better, it was just her teeth was fucked up. If Chunky would get her teeth fixed she would be alright, but I could work with her because her pussy was the bomb. I got up and got back in the shower and when I got out, Chunky was rolling the last of the weed up, she passed me the blunt and headed to the bathroom.

Chunky came out of the bathroom and laid down on the bed next to me.

"Chunky, get your ass up and get dressed, let's go to that bar before we hit the club."

"I need to go home because I don't have any clothes here," she said standing up grabbing her dress.

I put on the Gucci jogging suit and the Gucci shoes I had brought from the booster in the barber shop. I grabbed my gun, and Chunky and

I were out the door. I jumped behind the wheel of the minivan and drove to Chunky's house and waited in the van. Twenty minutes later she came back down in a loose-fitting one-piece Prada dress and some black Prada shoes; you can tell out the door she didn't have any panties on.

I got out of the van and got in the passenger seat because she was the driver. She sat her black Prada purse on the floor of the van. Chunky drove to the bar that was on Pulaski and Lake. It was an old looking bar that was in the cut, but there was nothing but new cars in the front. I told her to stay in the van while I got out and went into the bar. Once I walked in the bar, for some odd reason I felt like all eyes were on me. The bar was packed for it to be so early. I went to the bar and a tall, skinny red nigga with long braids came over and was just looking at me not saying shit.

"Can I get a double shot of Remy?" I asked pulling a twenty dollar bill out of my pocket.

He brought my drink and I was trying to decide if I should show him the picture or not. I decided not to show him the picture and just ask.

"Slim, I am looking for an old dude named Jamel, but they call him Melly. Do you know somebody by that name?" I asked, feeling all the eyes on me.

"Naw, I don't, but old Billy knows a lot of people, let me ask him do he know," Slim said walking off.

He went to some tall, dark skin old man that had bad skin, the old man looked down the bar at me and I saw him shaking his head no. So, I finished my drink and waited for the bartender to walk back down to me. He stopped to serve a couple of more people and then he came to me. He told me he didn't nobody know Melly and he walked off. When I looked down there where the old man was sitting he was gone. As I left the bar and went to the van, Chunky was just hanging up her phone as I approached.

"Go get some weed and hit the club you were telling me about." Chunky pulled off. "Chunky, where is the best weed in Chicago? That other weed was good, but I want that kill."

"I know some niggas on Lawndale and Thomas," she said heading that way.

Once we got there the block was packed. Chunky got out and instantly niggas were asking her what's up with Tony? When is Tony getting out? I was so busy in my thoughts that I forgot to give her the

21

money. When I was looking for her I couldn't find her because there were so many people on the block. Then she opened the door and got in taking the weed out of her purse.

"How much is it?" I asked going in my pocket.

"It's cool, I paid for it already," she said starting the car. But before she could pull off somebody was knocking on her window.

"Princess, let me have a cigarette," some short fat nigga asked. He had long dreads and he was bending down trying to see who I was.

"Boy, you know fucking well I don't smoke no fucking cigarettes," Chunky said raising up the window while pulling off and shaking her head.

"Who was that? And where are you getting this money from?" I asked thinking about my own funds getting low.

"That was Fat Man, remember the nigga Tony, the one I told you I was fucking with? That's one of his boys. Tony be over here and I be cracking credit cards. Plus, I was holding some of his money before he got locked up," she said pulling over at the gas station.

"How much money was you holding for Tony?" I asked going in my pocket and pulling out some money.

"It was around twenty-thousand, but I've been spending it," she said looking down.

I stepped out of the van to pay for the gas and get some blunts, but I really needed time to let my mind process what I just heard. On my way out, the gas station I seen a black Range Rover sport with smoke black windows just sitting there parked. It caught my eye because it was looking out of place. Just as quickly as I turned my attention back to this money that Chunky had, I pumped the gas thinking about my next move. I got back in the van and told Chunky to go to the club. While she was driving I reached over and put my hand under her dress and started rubbing her pussy. She started biting her lip and opening her legs at the same time.

She pulled up across the street from the club in a no parking zone while I rolled up blunt and we smoked. The weed was so strong I almost threw up. After we finished smoking I told her to pull into the parking lot and try to get as close to the door as possible. I had to leave my gun in the van because they were searching at the door. Chunky and I got out of the van and walked to the door. I paid one of the bouncers fifty-dollars to let us straight in the door. Once we got in the club we noticed it was packed. I walked over to the bar and Chunky was right behind me. I ordered two double shots of Remy and handed one to Chunky.

"Baby let me ask you something and keep it real. If that was your nigga, why when he got locked up you started fucking with me and spending his money?" I asked looking her in her eyes.

"Well, first, I wasn't his women. I was just some bitch to him, it was like we would go to the restaurant and he would see another bitch that was prettier than me and he would tell me to catch a cab home. Then she would jump in the car with him. He uses to always tell me I was ugly and wouldn't no nigga would want me; and about the money? He never mentioned it. To be honest, he may have forgotten because I've had it months before he got locked up," she said sipping her drink and looking around.

"What about me? What if I got lock up, are you going to fuck another nigga and leave me too?" I asked, trying to fill her out.

"As long as you want me, I'll be there. Just treat me right, please MJ," she said with tears running down her eyes.

"I am going to treat you right, I would never make you catch a cab if there was another female I wanted. I would just take you with us," I said in a joking way but meaning it.

She downed her drink, stepped on her tippy toes, kissed me on my cheek and went to the dance floor. I turned around and ordered another drink. Once the bartender came close enough I asked him if he knew my pops.

But he started laughing and said, "it's was too dark and too loud to know anybody in this club!"

So, I turned around and started looking for Chunky while sipping my drink. Ten minutes later I saw her walking through the crowd towards me with a slim, short, and pretty redbone with dreads and light brown eyes. Chunky walked up to me,

"MJ, this my friend Red, and Red this MJ." Chunky said standing on the side of me with Red standing in front of both of us.

I killed the drink I had in my hand and started rubbing on Chunky ass. While I was doing that I asked Red if she wanted something to drink, she said yeah and I turned to the bartender and asked if I could get a fifth of Remy. He told me yeah, for two-hundred and fifty dollars, so I handed him the two-fifty and asked for some cups. I handed Red the bottle and bent down and whispered in Chunky's ear.

"I want you to catch a cab home because I want to fuck her." She slapped me on my arm and told me to stop playing with her.

I grabbed the bottle from Red and poured Chunky some, then I turned my attention to Red. She had on a skirt so short I swear I could almost see her pussy. It was too dark to see what kind of dress it was... it was really too dark to see anything. Chunky handed me her cup and said she was going to the bathroom. There was only a little left in the cup so I downed it. Still holding the bottle in my hand, and while me and Red was standing there some nigga walked up and grabbed her hand and said, "what's up?" She snatched her hand away and leaned her ass against me, grabbed my arm and wrapping it around her saying, "don't you see I'm with my nigga?"

The guy said, "my fault homie," and walked away, but Red stayed there shaking her ass against my dick. By now, my dick was rock hard so I reached under her skirt and started rubbing her pussy, that made her start grinding harder against my dick. She turned around and started facing me and then she asked, "can I go with you tonight?"

"Chunky going with me," I said.

"Who?" she asked looking confused and I realized she didn't know Chunky.

"I mean Princess going with me."

"So, I still want to go," she said rubbing my dick.

"You have to ask Princess."

"Why do I have to ask her?" She asked sipping her drink.

"Because you're her friend and I am not going behind her back, but ask her and she might say yeah," I said.

When I turned to look for Chunky, she was standing right beside me.

"Where is my drink, MJ?" she asked smiling. I poured her some more in the cup and she grabbed Red's arm and started pulling her toward the dance floor.

Then she stopped and came back to kissed me on my cheek.

"You different and I respect you for including me the way you did." She turned around and grabbed Red's hand and they went to the dance floor.

I finished the fifth of Remy off and order another fifth. Chunky came back to the bar and leaned up against me with her ass on me facing the dance floor. She put her hand behind her back and slid it down my jogging pants and then started stroking my dick.

24

"Chunky you better stop before you get yourself in trouble," I whispered in her ear.

She turned around to faced me and I grabbed her around her waist, she was saying she was ready to go. Then Red came and wrapped her hands around Chunky's waist from the back and started putting her hand down my jogging pants. She whispered in Chucky's ear,

"Princess, can I go with you?"

"Yeah, you can go, I don't care," Chunky said.

Red took her hands out of my jogging pants and I felt her lift up Chunky's dress and start playing with her pussy. Chunky put her head on my chest and said she was ready to go.

"After we finish the bottle," I said pouring Red a little in a cup and telling her to drink it straight down.

She downed the cup and passed it to Chunky and said your turn. I poured Chunky some and she downed the drink. There was half a fifth left in the bottle and I was already fucked up. I hit the bottle hard and told Chunky fuck that, let's go. We started walking toward the door and Red was right on my heels. Chunky walked out the door first and Red was right behind me. I grabbed Red and pulled her in front of me and we walked toward the van.

Chunky popped the locks on the van and got in the front seat, I told Red to get in the front seat with Chunky and I pulled open the sliding door and that's when I noticed the black Range Rover parked next to our van. The back door of the Range opened up and I saw the gun coming down and felt my head explode, then everything went black.

Chapter (4)
- Chunky -

I *haven't been with this nigga but a week and he got me going crazy. I never been with a female before, but this is going to tell if this my nigga or not. I know this bitch Red want my nigga because she can't keep her hands off him, but it's cool, we are going to see what's up…* I was thinking on our way to the van. And as I was getting in, out of nowhere two niggas jumped out of a black **Range Rover** and hit **MJ** over the head with a gun. They pulled him into the back of the Range Rover and pulled off.

"What the fuck just happened?" Red asked rising up from the floor of the minivan holding her heart.

My hands were shaking so bad I couldn't get the key in the ignition. I finally got the keys in and pulled out of the parking lot and the Range Rover was gone. I looked at Red confused, wondering where to go and what to do. I headed toward the hotel hoping that my phone would started ringing, hoping this was some kind of joke. I had the key to the room so I pulled up to the room and ran inside, but nobody was there. So, I came back out after grabbing the weed and rolled up a blunt.

"Red, do you want me to take you home?"

"Girl, I am not leaving you out here by yourself," Red said looking around.

"Let's sit in the van and smoke until we hear something," I said lighting the weed.

*　　　*　　　*

- MJ -

I woke up and I was in a basement tied to a chair. I could feel blood all over my face and I had something over my head. I could hear people talking all around me. I didn't know who these niggas were. *I know fucking well Bear didn't track me down all the way to Chicago or could it be that clown that I shot? I am not saying shit or answering shit until I find out who these niggas are…* I was thinking. Suddenly, when someone snatched something off my head and I see three niggas standing around me. One was a tall, clean-cut nigga with light brown skin. There there was an older nigga with dark skin and he had a mean look on his face, and there was a young nigga. I could see the hood in the young nigga eyes, he was around six feet, but this nigga had a smile on his face.

"So, let's make this quick because I have something to do," the young nigga said bending down to look me in my eyes. "So, who the fuck is you?"

I didn't say shit. I just looked around the room, then out of nowhere he punched me in my jaw and bent down again.

"Who the fuck sent you?" he asked looking at me. I said nothing again.

"Look, Nico, hand me that knife since this nigga don't want to talk. I'm going to cut his fucking tongue out of his fucking mouth."

The clean-cut nigga who name I just figured out was name Nico handed him a knife.

"Is this bitch even sharp?" The young nigga asked Nico swiping the knife across my arm cutting through my shirt and cutting open my upper arm like a knife through butter. Blood instantly went running down my arm.

"Dino, grab him around the neck so I can cut this nigga tongue out his mouth," the young nigga said looking at me with a smile on his face.

The old dark skin nigga grabbed me around my neck and pulled my head back with so much force that I knew I was in trouble if I didn't say something.

"What do you want to know?" I manage to get out of my mouth.

"Who sent you?" The young nigga asked looking at me with eyes of a killer.

"Nobody sent me, what do you mean?"

"What's your name?"

"MJ."

But before he could ask me anything else my phone started ringing. He cut straight down my leg through my jogging pants cutting my pocket open, and everything fell out of my pocket. He bent down and picked up my phone, and for the first time I noticed that there was somebody behind me because they moved and picked up something that had fallen out of my pocket. The somebody that was behind me spoke for the first time.

"Look young blood, I am going to ask you once and only once, so you better think about your answer because this answer will determine if you live or if you die. Now, how did you get this picture, the one that was in your pocket?"

"My mother gave it to me," I said somehow knowing he was the boss of these guys.

"Who is your mother, and why did she give you this picture?" He asked.

"My mother's name was Debra and she wanted me to find my father who is in the picture," I said.

Then the lights came on and the man came from behind me and looked me in my eyes; he shook his head while walking away and said,

"Demar, cut him loose and clean him up, then bring him upstairs.

"Pops what?" said Demar.

I found out the young nigga name was Demar. The man stopped and turned around, then looked at the young wild nigga and said,

"Demar, meet your brother," and walked off.

Demar looked at me, and now I was smiling, then he looked at Dino and Nico shaking his head.

"What the fuck is going on?" Then he cut me loose.

*   *   *

Demar threw me a towel and walked off going up a set of stairs. I followed feeling like my head was about to come off. When I got upstairs my father was pacing back and forth in a black suit, white shirt with no tie, and a shoulder holster with a chrome 1911 45.

"Pops, what's going on and where did he come from?" Demar asked Pops as he walked over to the bar in the corner and poured himself a drink.

"Demar not now! Call Dr. Brown and tell him to get over here A.S.A.P to patch him up. And I want everybody to leave us alone," he said walking to the bar.

"So, he staying Pops?" Demar asked, eyes and mouth wide open looking from me to pops.

"What the fuck do you mean is he staying, boy this is your fucking brother!" Pop's said, with a look on his face that would scare a bear.

Then Demar threw a set of keys in my lap,

"You just bought yourself a new Range Rover since you got all that blood in my back seat," he said walking towards the door.

I managed to say, through a sore jaw and a busted head, "I don't have any money for a Range Rover."

"Don't worry, you're good for it. Remember, Pops said you're staying." And with that he left out the door leaving me and Pops.

"Go clean yourself up and we'll talk, and some clothes are in one of the rooms back there that you should be able to fit," he said pouring himself another drink.

I got up and left the room walking down a long hallway. The floors were marble, the ceiling was high and all the walls were white; it looked like it was around five-bedroom in this house. I found the master bedroom in the back of the house and went in the bathroom. The shower was bigger than me and mom's whole bathroom. As I got in, I noticed the shower had ten shower heads coming from everywhere. I stepped through the glass door and turned the water on as hot as it would get and just sat there letting the water run over my body. I had been looking for my father and now that I found him what was I going to do? I was thinking while the water rolled down my body.

I washed up and as I stepped out of the shower there was a black man with wrinkles in his face and a gray beard, he was sitting in a chair holding a medical bag.

"I am Dr. Brown," he said as I came out the shower wrapped in a towel.

"Give me a minute," I said turning. For the first time I noticed the walk-in closet. I walked in and it looked like a fucking clothes store, and most of the clothes still had tags on them. I grabbed a pack of boxers off the stack that was sitting on the shelf. I put the boxers on and went in the room with Dr. Brown. As I walked in the room a little blood ran down my face and I wiped it away walking towards Dr. Brown.

"Sit down on the bed and let me look at your cuts," he said opening his medical bag. He looked at the cut and said you're going to need stitches. He took out a needle and some thread and started sewing up my leg. He put eight stitches in my leg, then ten in my head, and put six in my arm. After he was done, I jumped in the shower again and rinsed the blood off me. Dr. Brown put some cream on the stitches and wrapped them up.

I grabbed a pair of Giorgio Armani jeans and t-shirt, and went down the hall to where my pops was sitting. He was sitting on the couch with a drink in his hand. As soon as I walked in the room he turned to me.

"How did Debra die? Downstairs you said your mother name was Debra." I knew right then and there that pops was sharp and he listened to everything.

"She died of cancer," I said and watched his eyes moist.

"Did she ever have more kids?"

"No, she died alone and she told me to tell you sorry," I said standing up and walking to the bar to pour myself a drink.

My pops and I talked and I learned a lot. I found out that he cheated on my mom and she cheated with one of his friends, then stole $100,000 dollars and left. But he had already new she was pregnant before this because he found her papers. She tried to hide, he had been looking for my mom for years. I told him mom had not been with another man, and that she traveled from city to city never staying one place two long. He told me I was at home and not to worry any longer. He said I could stay here for tonight and he would take me somewhere more comfortable in the morning.

I told him I had all my things at the hotel, he gave me a credit card and told me he had to go but he'll be back in the morning. He said I could call a cab and he gave me the pin number to the card. He told me I was in Logan Square and that he was sorry for everything, his eyes were moist. The last thing he said before leaving was that I'll meet everybody tomorrow and he was sorry, again.

* * *

- *Chunky* -

I'd been calling MJ's phone back to back but no answer. We had smoked almost all the weed and drunk the rest of the Remy that was in the bottle. Red wouldn't let me drop her off at home and I had made up my mind that if I didn't talk to MJ in two days I was calling the cops. It was almost morning so I parked the van and Red and I went into the room. I was really stressing about MJ and didn't know what to do, but this bitch Red acted like she don't give a fuck and it was pissing me off. As soon as we got in the room Red took all her clothes off and laid on the bed. I told her I had to get something out of the van and I grabbed MJ's bookbag with all his clothes and put it in the van.

Then I went back in the room and this bitch was watching porn, I ran back out to the van and grabbed one of MJ's t-shirts. I went into the bathroom and took off my clothes and put on the t-shirt and got into the bed and started calling MJ.

* * *

- *MJ* -

I had called a cab, but I had forgotten the address so I went out in the front to look at the address and I see the black Range Rover in the driveway. I went back inside to get the keys and found some paper and pen, I wrote down the address and jumped in the range. The first thing I did was look in the back seat, there was blood in the back seat but it wasn't that bad. Then I grabbed my phone and turned it back on because Demar had turned it off. Once my phone booted up I searched for the Mark Twain hotel. When the address popped up I put the navigation in the truck and pulled off.

While I was driving I dropped the phone on the floor and the phone slid under the seat, and as soon as it went under the seat it started ringing. I pulled up to a red light and started reaching under the seat for the phone, but the light turned green and I pulled off. I was only twenty minutes from the hotel, so I said fuck it and kept driving. Once I pulled up at the hotel and saw the minivan, I parked behind it and jumped out, when I made it to the lobby I told the man behind the counter I lost my key. He recognized who I was and gave me another key card. I went to my room and when I opened the door I was surprised to see Red laying there naked and Chunky had on one of my t-shirts, they both were asleep.

Light was coming through the hotel window and I saw Chunky's purse on the floor, I grabbed her purse and went through it looking for the weed. I found the weed rolled up in a blunt and blazed up. While smoking, I looked out the window and watched the sun rise. I put my hand under Chunky's t-shirt and rubbed on her pussy and she slapped my hand away saying Red stop. I did it again and when she sat up and saw me she just started crying. I put my hand to her mouth and told Chunky to be quiet and come outside of the room. I grabbed a towel out of the bathroom and was looking for my bookbag when Chunky grabbed me pulling me out the room door.

"What's wrong, why didn't you want me to wake up Red? Did she have something to do with this?" She asked rubbing the band aids on my head.

"No, she was cool, but I just wanted to see you," I said walking with her to the front door of the hotel. Chunky looked out the front door of the hotel and saw the Range Rover and started pulling me, and hollering telling me come on there they go again! I grabbed her and told her I was driving the Range and she started asking me a whole lot of questions, but I stopped her and told her I would explain everything to her later, once I found out what's going on.

"Where's my book bag?"

"I put everything in the van because I was going to take them home." I told Chunky that

"Look, I have to handle something for a few days. You can go home or you could stay here because it was still paid for," I explained.

"I'll stay, but if I leave I'm at home."

I kissed Chunky and told her to open the door to the van so I can grab the bookbag.

"Keep the van."

I left heading back to Logan Square to talk to pops and meet everybody like he said.

Chapter (5)
- MJ -

I pulled back up to the house in Logan Square. Pops was parked in the front setting in a banged-up Ford F-150 with light tint. Once I parked the Range he waved me over to come to the truck.

"Son, come take a ride with me," he said looking like a construction worker. He saw the way I was looking at him when I got into the truck because he instantly said, "Sometimes it's not always good to shine. Son, there's a lot of things that we have to do and a lot of things we have to talk about, but first, I want you to know your mother was my one and only true love. Now, I have loved before her and after her, but she was my true love. Hopefully, you don't take this the wrong way, I know you look like me and I could see myself in you. But, I still need a DNA test, and sometime later down the line I'll explain that to you. MJ, there is a lot going on in our family right now and I don't want you to get caught up in somebody else's bullshit. I'm not going to play games or hide anything from you, there's a war. A drug war that's been going on over turf and we're getting hit on all sides. Plus, we have somebody in our organization that's playing both sides," he said looking older by the minute.

"I want in, put me in the organization."

"MJ, it always hurts more to have and lost, than to not have in the first place," Pops said looking at me.

"I don't understand what that means?"

"Well, I'll give you an example: If I were to lose everything I have it would hurt, but if I never had it I wouldn't know what it was like to lose it." He said trying to see if I understood.

"That's a chance I am willing to take," I said and meant every word.

Pops pulled off and jumped on the expressway while we talked, he told me I had three uncle's, three brothers and one sister. Everybody was doing their own thing, but under one roof which meant he was the boss. My sister, whose name was Tasha, ran all the legit parts of the business and she stayed out the way, rarely coming around. My brother Nico, controlled the south part of Chicago, and Demar the north. I knew he meant drugs, but Demar was wild as hell - always starting trouble and always so flashy. Nico was the total opposite. He was laid back, and never starting trouble, but both were quick to finish it.

Then there were my uncles. I heard Dino, who I've already met, was an old aggressive, and territorial manipulator who was Bear watching. Next, there was Flight, a quiet man who stayed to himself and didn't socialize very much. He also stayed out of trouble. And then, there was Ronald who wanted to be known as Boss, he and his two sons wanted to take over the organization. Now finally, Curtis, or rather Curty-P, who's ambitious and has an army, but once he gets drunk he'll go to war with anybody over anything.

"Now, do you still want a part of this?" He asked driving not taking his eyes off the road.

"Damn, well…" but before I could speak Pops said.

"MJ, a man always speaks his mind."

"Well, if all this is happening, why are you still in it?" I asked.

"Because I'm in too deep. Plus, at the end of the day we're all family, and family comes before everything. Family first, fuck friends and don't forget that." He said taking his eyes off the road and looking me straight in my eyes.

We drove in silence for the next thirty minutes and we got off the exit in Wisconsin. We drove ten more minutes until we came to a back road that led to a house that looked like it was out of a movie. Like one of them big old plantation houses in slave movies. Once we went through the gates it took us five more minutes to make it to the house.

"Why are you driving this old broken-down looking truck?" I asked looking around the estate.

"Because the light that shines the brightest gets put out first," he said pulling to a stop at the house.

There was nothing but Range Rovers, Audis, Lexus, BMWs parked out front. I guess the family has made it…

"And remember this before we go in here, a boy who won't stand for himself, becomes a man who can't stand up to anything." He jumps out the truck with me trailing behind him.

*   *   *

We got out of the truck and started walking towards the house when an old man about seventy came to the door.

"Good morning Mr. Jones, everyone's in the conference room," he said as me and pops walked past the old man.

Inside the house it was like something I had never seen before, marble floors, white furniture, vase's, fresh flowers everywhere and maids and butlers running around everywhere. It also had chandeliers, we walked down a hallway and into a room where seven people were sitting around a round table. In the middle of the table there were two F's engraved upside down, but facing each other and around the edge of the table was 'Family First Fuck Friends' written over and over in gold letters. When we walked in a tall nigga was sitting at the table, who I would later find out name was Flight was the first to speak.

"I was going to ask you who was that, but I could see it's your son because he looks like you twenty years ago." After he spoke he started laughing, sipping his drink.

Pops sat down at the table and I sat in the only empty seat left.

"Boy, that's not your seat, that's Tasha's seat, what do you think you're doing?" My uncle Boss Ron snapped, but before I could respond pops spoke up.

"Ron, he's in, and it's still going to be Tasha's seat," he said looking around the table.

"So, if he's getting in, where is he going to work because we have Chicago already sewn up. Demar has the North, Nico have the South, Boss Ron has the 100's, Flight has from Oak park to Cicero, Curty-P has Northwest and Humboldt Park, and I got out west, so where is he going to work?" Dino asked looking at Pops.

"He can take my area downtown," Pops said looking around.

"What about when what's his name…" Boss-Ron was saying, but before he could finish Pops jumped up and hit the table with both hands shaking the drinks on the table.

"He's in! End of story! Now, how's everything else going otherwise?" Pops said looking around.

I found out that we were into it with the Jamaicans on the Northside, and the Latino's in Humboldt Park. Then I learned that Pops handed out work and every month on the first the bills were due, meaning you had to pay for the work that you got. Nobody sold heroin because it made you too hot. After about thirty minutes, everybody got up to leave. Nico was the first to walk up to me and say congratulation and welcome to the family bro, then he hugged me around my back.

35

Everybody started coming up to congratulate me. After that, they left and once again it was Pops and I.

"Don't take this the wrong way thinking I am not grateful because I am, but from what I saw downtown it's really for working people and partying," I said looking confused.

"That's what everybody thinks, but you'll work the club because after all the dope boys make their money they go downtown to party. You just need your people that will not stand out. Plus, I have a condo downtown that you could use until you decide what you want to do. Now, you're going to have to mingle and rub shoulders with some of these people to get your feet wet, and always remember when rubbing shoulders and mingling, the most powerful impression a person can make is that they don't care if they make an impression," Pops said walking out the conference room. "This is your house to make yourself at home," Pops said over his back.

It was almost one o'clock so I called Chunky and told her to keep Red around because I had a job for her, then she told me she was about to drop Red off because she kept trying to fuck her. I told her that was good and to let her, what could it hurt... then I hung up.

*　　*　　*

- *Chunky* -

I was getting ready to get up and drop this bitch Red off when MJ called and said to keep her around, and to basically let Red eat my pussy. Now, I've fucked with females before but never my friends, but for some reason I said fuck it. I jumped up and got in the shower while Red was still laying down naked, when I got out of the shower I walked in the room with the towel wrapped around my chest and barely covering my ass and pussy. I went over and bent down in front of Red going into my purse to get my lotion. Once I bent over, I already knew my ass and pussy was hanging from under the towel, then I grabbed my lotion and walked over to the bed and took the towel off as begin to put the lotion on.

Red was watching me so I asked her if she could put some lotion on my back, she said yeah and told me to lay down on my stomach as she started rubbing lotion on my back and all the way down to my ass. Once she was finished with my backside she told me to turn around so she could do the front, so I turned around and laid on my back and she instantly started kissing on my tits moving her way down to my stomach. I started moaning to let her know it was feeling good, then she started moving down and begin to kiss my pussy lightly; I started moaning trying to push her head down, but she started kissing between my legs on my thighs and rubbing on my titties at the same time. Then this bitch Red started lightly blowing on my pearl tongue and rubbing her fingers against my pussy, I wanted her to put her fingers in my pussy so bad it was driving me crazy.

Next, she put her tongue on my pearl tongue and started putting her fingers in my pussy at the same time, I was already horny and wet by then so I instantly start cumming, but she didn't stop. Instead, she covered my pearl tongue with her mouth and started sucking my pearl tongue while she moved two fingers in and out of my pussy at the same time. Before I knew what was going on I started cumming again. When Red finished, I could do nothing but curl up and go to sleep.

Chapter (6)
- MJ -

After I got off the phone with Chunky, I took a nap, and when I woke up from my nap it was 5pm. I went walking around the house and found Pops in the kitchen eating a steak and baked potato. I had the chef make me a double bacon burger; and while me and Pops ate, he explained to me what I needed to do. He told me to play the clubs. They're dark, loud, and there will always be a lot of people so I wouldn't have to worry about a wire or being recorded. He gave me the club 'The Hot Spots' on Michigan and State, and right across the street he had a condo. I was going to have to hit the bouncers, but everything should be cool.

Pops told me he had a couple of customers already that he had been dealing with that I could have. He also told me that I needed a female to move with me to keep a low profile, and make sure we both look like money. With that said we both got up and left walking towards the front door, he told me he was about to take me to the condo and I was prepared to see the old truck. But out front was a 2019 Audi truck, gray with smoke black windows, Pops jumped in the driver seat and on our way to the condo he explained that he was giving me five bricks of cocaine at $20,000 a piece, but he was letting them go for $32,000.

I was deep in thought when Pops pulled up to a high rise building and the valet said,

"Good afternoon Mr. Jones, how are you doing?"

Pops got out of the car and said to the velvet, "This my son, he'll be staying here for a while," and we walked off.

We went to the elevator and Pops put a card in the elevator and hit the P button for Penthouse and as we got off the elevator we were in the house. It was one big room with windows going all the way around. There was a sunken living room with white leather furniture. Then there was a chef's kitchen, but the crazy part was the bedroom. There was a California king size bed, 80-inch TV on the wall with windows all around the room, plus there was a walk-in closet with a master bathroom. The closet had a couple of suits in there and I was so caught up in the house that I didn't even see the bookbag in his hand.

"These are your five, and I'll talk to the security guard and the front desk to let them know you're here. If you don't understand or need to know anything, call." And then Pops handed me a new phone that was just for him and he was gone.

I sat in the bedroom looking out the window thinking to myself - just 72 hours ago I didn't know my father and now, I was in a Penthouse with two trucks. Shit was going well. It was 7pm so I grabbed the key card Pops had left me and shot out the door. When I got downstairs I saw the valet and asked for the truck. He told me the next time just call and he'll have the truck ready. Five minutes later I was driving towards the hotel to see Chunky. It took me thirty-minutes to get to the hotel and I felt like I was in a spaceship.

As I pulled up and parked, I noticed the minivan hasn't been moved. I walked in and the front desk gave me another key card and I went down the hall and opened the door. When I saw Red she jumped up and came running to me asking if I was okay. I looked over to Chunky and she had not moved. Red was standing in front of me naked, then she said,

"Yeah, I put her to sleep…" Smiling, I slapped Red on the ass and said good girl and walked over to Chunky and slap her on her ass as well, but she just rolled over. I don't know what it was, and it could have been from seeing both of them naked, but my dick was hard as hell so I went to the drawer and grabbed one of the rubbers that I left there and told Red to bend over the chair in the room. I pulled down my pants and put the rubber on and started slapping my dick against Red's pussy making sure she was wet, once I knew she was wet I put my dick in and to my surprise Red's pussy was tight as hell. I was pulling my dick all the way out, but the tip was still in, then I'll go all the way back until my balls hit her ass cheeks, real slow.

Red's pussy was leaking and she was biting her arm, then I started speeding up and she started squirting cum everywhere. Then I started pounding her out. She was cumming so much that it was getting all over my stomach. Red jumped up and was sitting on the chair looking at me. She said she couldn't finish and took the rubber off and sucked my dick until I nutted. When she finished, I jumped in the bed with my clothes on and started shaking Chunky trying to get her up. She finally woke up and threw her arms around me when she saw it was me and started hugging me. I told Chunky to roll up the little weed that was left and told Red to get her ass over here.

She got off the chair and started walking toward the bed and I saw she was still cumming. Red got on the bed and after Chunky finished rolling up the weed we smoked and talked. I found out Red didn't have a nigga and that she was 22 years old, and she stayed with her mom. She had a brother who sold drugs on the north side and he also took care of her. She and Chunky went to school together. First, I asked Chunky what she wanted and she said she wanted me, then I asked Red the same thing and she just looked down. I told her to be honest and she honestly told me what she wanted.

"I want the both of you," Red said keeping her head down.

"Since nobody asked me what I wanted, I want the both of you, but I don't want no jealous kid shit. I want loyalty because like yesterday anything could happen. I want us to be more than a team, but a family a real family, and I don't care about neither one of your pussy, not more than your mind and loyalty. So, if this is something you don't think you could accept I understand, but hopefully we could still be friends and if you don't want to do this let me know now. If we are together, to be disloyal is punishable by death," I explained looking them both in the eyes.

Red was the first to say that's what she always wanted, then Chunky looked at me and started crying.

"I take loyalty very seriously because I know how it feels to always give out loyalty but never receive it. So, baby I'll be more loyal to you then any creature under the sun," Chunky said looking me in the eyes.

I looked at her and felt her truth. I looked at Red and Chunky and said, "this makes you sisters no matter what, and always know she has your best interest in mind, and beware of jealousy because it's a dangerous thing. Don't ever trust no one then."

I went on to explain how we're going to go to the club to party and meet people. Both of them knew about drugs so it was about them pointing out the dope boys and the stick-up kids. Then I told them to grab their shit and let's go.

Once we stepped out of the hotel door, Chunky was looking for the Range Rover and when she didn't see it she popped the locks to the van. But when I told her we're driving in the Audi, I saw the look of surprise on her face. I told her to direct me to get to the weed on Lawndale and Thomas, and once we got over there I told Chunky to get two ounces of weed. I handed her $400 from the money I took from Bear. As she got out I was looking around and there were to many people to be just weed out there. When she came back I was about to say something, but instead I made a mental note of it.

"Red, have you two ate anything yet?" I asked her as Chunky was getting back in the truck.

"Naw, I haven't eaten any food, but I ate Chunky," she said laughing as me and her clapped hands over the back seat.

"Fuck both of you," Chunky said putting the weed in her purse. I pulled off and we went to Portillos and grabbed us something to eat. After we got our food I shot to the condo and we jumped out and the valet parked the truck. Red and Chunky was looking back and forth at each other, but once we got on the elevator and I pushed P for Penthouse Chunky said,

"Okay, you taking us to the bat cave."

When the door opened we were in the condo, Chunky and Red went running around the crib going crazy, hollaring from room to room.

"Girl, come look at this view…

"girl looked at the kitchen…"

I grabbed the bottle of Louis Xlll off the bar in the front room and sat down and poured me a drink. I heard Red calling Chunky girl.

"Did you see that shower in their bathroom?"

"Naw, where?"

"In the master bedroom, come on let's get in."

Taking off her clothes running to the room, Chunky went in behind Red and two cups and thirty minutes later they both came out naked walking into the front room.

"Where is our food?" Chunky asked looking at me.

"In the kitchen," I said walking into the bathroom and jumping in the shower myself wondering if I was making the right move by bringing them here.

When I walked out of the shower into the room where Red and Chunky was laying in the bed rolling up weed. With just a towel around me I looked out the window at the city, I grabbed the Louis-Xlll and hit it straight out of the bottle and I felt my body relaxing. I laid in the bed and thought about my plans for the morning. Things were about to go down.

* * *

I woke up to the bed moving and Red eating Chunky's pussy, I jumped out the bed and went into the kitchen to look in the refrigerator, then went back in the room.

"One of you freaky bitches go cook breakfast," I said watching Chunky eyes roll in the back of her head from the head Red was giving her.

Red jumped up and started for the kitchen while I grabbed one of the blunts from last night and sparked it up and went in the front room to call Pops. He answered on the second ring.

"Boy I was just about to call you, look, I got somebody that's going to come meet you at the club. Plus, I forgot to tell you about the truck. Once you get in there put the truck in neutral, hit the brakes and turn the left blinker on, and before I forget, I gave that number to your uncles and brothers," he said without taking a breath.

"Okay, but I was calling to see how much I could spend off the card that you gave me,"

"It doesn't matter, go into the store and have some fun," he said hanging up the phone.

I went into the kitchen and Red had cooked bacon, eggs, rice, and toast. We ate, I grabbed my weed, and we were out the door while Red and Chunky was asking where we were going. Once the valet pulled the truck around I did what my Pops told me to do and the floor in the back seat opened up revealing a brick, a .50 caliber desert eagle with an extended clip, plus a nine. I pushed the slot close and drove the truck to the water tower and we got out to tear the mall up.

First store we went in, Red grabbed an all-white Fendi bodysuit, with the legs on the bodysuit cut into shorts, logo Fendi going down each arm, one white and the other one blue. Also a pair of boots that came above the knee with Fendi going down the side. Red got a pair of red bottoms to go with her bodysuit. Then Chunky got a Versace summer dress that was tight around the top but lose at the bottom with a pair of flat Versace shoes, she also got two dresses from Dolce and Gabbana with the shoes to match.

Red got two Prada outfits with the shoes to match, and I hit the Gucci store. I got a lean short set with Gucci all white across the arms with all white Gucci shoes, bally style with a Gucci hat, watch, and an all-black leather Gucci jacket with Gucci across the back that cost $6,000.

Then I got two Balenciaga fits with the shoes. We left the mall spending almost $25,000, but on our way out the mall Chunky said she need a purse, so we went back to the Fendi store. She got a Fendi back pack purse, and while we were in there I seen two niggas tearing the store up, I turned to Red and she instantly said those were the twins, they be out south, these niggas are getting money.

"Do you know them?" I asked her.

"Yeah, they cool… one of my girls got a baby by the one with the dreads," she said waving to the one in the dreads.

"Red, introduced them to me, I need to see what's up on the work and introduce me as your cousin," I said pushing Red into that direction.

She went over and introduced us, and I told homie I had some work for the low; and he asked what were my numbers.

"$28,000, money back guaranteed," I threw out there.

"I'll hit you in a day or two to check one out," he said, and we exchanged numbers and left the mall.

"I think I might know somebody that might get some work," Chunky said looking at me.

"Who?" I said while driving down State.

"My sister's baby daddy, he was selling drugs across the street from the store we met at."

"Show me how to get over there and you could go holla at him," I said getting directions from Chunky.

Once we got in the parking lot, she called her sister, and this fat nigga with long dreads and a diamond chain around his neck that said 'Dope Boy' walked over to the truck as I was getting out.

"What's up homie, you got some butter?"

"Yeah, I got something, I have them for $27,000."

"Man, that's cheap, is the shit any good?" He asked looking around.

"Bro, it's always money back guarantee."

"Well, how long will it take you to bring me one so I could see what it does? And if it's right, I'll be fucking with you, and what's your name?"

"My name MJ, and give me like twenty minutes and I'll be parked right here," I said stepping in the truck.

"Okay, I'll be ready," the buyer said and walk off.

I pulled off and went to the gas station down the street and filled up the tank and popped the secret slot and left it open, I rolled up a blunt and passed it to Red and told her to blaze. We smoked the blunt and when I pulled back up he was sitting on the hood of a Dodge Charger, Fat boy waved me over and I jumped out and grabbed the 9mm. and the brick, and walked to the black charger with tinted windows and got in.

"By the way, what's your name?" I asked fat boy and he looked at me pointing at his chain like I was supposed to know.

"Dope Boy," he said passing me a bag with money in it.

I took the money out the bag and started counting it and before I finished counting the money I handed the work to him and then finished.

"Man, if this shit is good I'll be back to holla at you today or tomorrow," he said tasting the work.

Once I finished counting the money I jumped out and jumped back in the truck and put the money and the gun back in the slot and closed it. I pulled off having made my first sell and I was on hundred and the only thing I knew is I wanted another sell. "Man, we are about to celebrate, what do y'all want to do?" I asked looking at Red.

"Let's pop an x-pill?" She said looking at Chunky.

"I don't care, it's up to him," Chunky said looking at Red.

"Well, Red came up front and drive," I said pulling over and jumping in the back seat.

Red jumped in the front seat and we shot somewhere out west, Chunky rolled down her window and asked who had the pills, and some young nigga came up to the car.

"How many babies?" one asked.

"Can I get three for the fifty?" Chunky asked pulling out fifty dollars, "and they're flats right?" she asked grabbing the pills and handing him the money.

Red pulled off and we shot to the crib to change and get ready to hit the club. It was still early and Chunky said I needed to put something in my stomach before I popped the pill, so we ordered a pizza. We ate, showered, and chilled in the bed talking up until 9:00pm, then got dressed. I grabbed two bricks, the weed and then called downstairs to tell them to have the truck ready. When we walked off the elevator the truck was in front of the building. While walking to the truck, I handed Chunky the bookbag and went into my pocket and handed the valet a fifty-dollar bill. We jumped in the truck and shot to the club.

We went to the 'Red Light' first, I put a brick in the secret slot and we were out the truck. Chunky and Red knew the bouncers so we went right to the front of the line and nobody searched us. Once inside the club, I went to the bar while Red and Chunky hit the dance floor to mingle around. I ordered a fifth of Remy and watched Red, she had put on an all black lace see through bodysuit by Tom Ford, and Chunky had on the white Fendi bodysuit, with the Fendi boots. Her bodysuit was so tight you could see her pussy print perfectly. They were on the dance floor and them niggas was going crazy. Chunky came over to where I was standing and asked if I wanted to take the pill yet. I said not yet because we were going to another club. She took a sip of my drink and went back to the dance floor.

Red came over to the bar and her pussy was so fat I had to rub it, "you don't have any panties on, do you?" I asked rubbing on her pussy.

"Boy naw, and you better stop before you make my pussy leak all over this suit," she said stepping back. "I came over here to tell you the nigga Shine is in the building, he's one of them Jamaicans from the north side, remember when I told you I use to fuck with one of the Jamaicans… well, he's the boss. I'm going to holla at him, but I think you should send him a drink to V.I.P," she said trying to see what I was going to do. I told her I was going to send over a bottle and she walked off. I ordered a bottle and after I sent it, he waved me over. I came over and Red introduced us.

"My name MJ, and my girl told me about you. I was trying to meet with you to do business."

"My name Shine, and what do you have in mind?"

"I got some cocaine that's 90% pure, and I'm letting them go for $28,000," I said seeing what he would say.

"That's a good price, but what if I came and copped ten or better?" he asked sipping his drink.

"I could drop the price to $26,500 each."

"Could you give me one on my name and if it's what you say it is I'll be back tomorrow to grab the other nine."

"Yeah, that's cool," I said standing up.

"My people will meet you wherever you want," Shine said pulling out his phone. We exchanged numbers and I told some big guy with dreads to meet me outside in ten minutes, and then I left to go to the truck.

I was sitting in the truck when I saw Shine's guy come out the club. I hit the lights and he came over and got in the truck. After I handed him the brick he jumped out and went to a white Range Rover before pulling off. I grabbed my phone and called pops, "Pops, how long will it take if I needed ten dollars?"

"I see you're finding your way, they'll be there in the morning… just be at home," he said hanging up.

Before I could get out the car my phone rang again, and it sounded like ole dude, he said his name was Shawn and that Melly told him to call me. We agreed to meet at the gas station down the street in an hour, and then I hung up. I put the money in the secret slot and got out the truck and went back into the club. When I made it back in the club Red was at the bar holding the bottle and Chunky was on the dance floor. Shine looked over at me and gave me the thumbs up sign and I told Red to get Chunky because we were about to leave after the drink.

Red came back with Chunky and as soon as Chunky came close I reach down and rubbed on her pussy. Chunky opened her legs and told Red to pass the cup, we killed the bottle and left the club. Once we got into the truck I told Chunky to roll a blunt to kill time because we were about to meet up with Shawn. We smoked the blunt and was about to roll up another one when Shawn called, he was pulling up at the gas station. So, I pulled off and pulled into the gas station. When I got there, it was an old man around sixty with a gray bread, so I called Shawn's phone and I saw the old man pick up the phone.

"Go sit in the car, somebody will be right over in white," I said popping the secret slot and taking out the brick. I handed the brick to Chunky, "just grab the money and come right back, don't worry about counting it yet because we don't know what Pops charged him."

As Chunky stepped out the truck I told Red to go grab some waters and make sure you watch out for Chunky. I handed Red some money and she got out the truck and walked into the gas station watching Chunky, along with the old man. Chunky got out of the car and came over to the truck and jumped in.

"That old man was in the car trying to get my number, with his freaky ass," Chunky said handing me the money.

I put the money in the secret slot and got in the back seat. Red came back out and handed me the water as she jumped in the driver's seat and we pulled off heading to the club the 'Hot Spot.'

Chapter (7)
- Demar -

Demar road through the Northside of Chicago in his Bentley coupe looking over his blocks. He was the only person on the Northside selling heroin and he made sure of that. (Everybody sold cocaine but nobody was going to sell heroin), Demar was thinking when his phone rang.

"Yeah, what's going on Dino?"

"It's about time to re-up, but we're going to have to make sure your Pops has his money also," Dino was saying before Demar cut him off.

"Look, bring me what you got and let me worry about him, and what's up with that nigga MJ, have you heard anything about him?"

"Naw, I don't think he's got his feet wet yet."

"Okay, just go to the spot and drop that off," I said hanging up.

Pops was talking about don't sell heroin, but this shit was moving and that's what the people wanted. I had taken the money from the work that Pops had given Dino and I, and I bought some heroin and there was no looking back. Pops was giving us twenty-five bricks of cocaine, every month for twenty-three thousand each so our bill every month was $575,000. Dino and I put our bill money together and the Cuban give us thirty bricks of uncut heroin for $1,000,000 dollars. Now, we were going to get sixty bricks of heroin for $2,000,000. I called some of my shorties and told them to meet me at the spot.

I pulled on Dover and Leland and got out of the Bentley, Tay Boogie and Gotti were waiting on me - they were some of my shorty's that was down for anything. I had met Tay at this bitch crib out south in Moe town. I was fucking this bitch I had met at the club one night and Tay Boogie was in the next room fucking her sister. The next thing I know both of their niggas was knocking on the door and we had to shoot our way out of there and Tay Boogie been on the team ever since. Then I met Gotti at a strip club, they were my two main shorty and I had a crew of these young niggas.

"That nigga Dino just went upstairs with a big ass bag," Tay Boogie said laughing giving me dap. We went upstairs and Dino was on the phone, but he pointed to the bag.

47

"Dino, I'm about to go make that move so I'll holla at you tomorrow," I said leaving Dino as I called Frank, the Cuban connect. "Frank, are you ready for me?" I asked grabbing the blunt from Tay Boogie.

"Yeah, I'll meet you in an hour at the gas station right off the e-way."

"I'll be in a black van and make sure it's the pure gray, and it has to be 100%," I said before hanging up. "Gotti, bring the van around front."

I went in the back room and grabbed three Draco's with the 100-round drum. Tay Boogie grabbed two and we went downstairs to jump in the van. Frank was one of Pop's friends and he knew that Pops didn't like the heroin so he kept everything on the low, but for the last six months I've been flooding the streets with that pure uncut heroin, nobody could compete. I had started giving bricks to Donnie and - Jermaine on the low. They were Boss Ron's two sons, it was time for the young niggas to take over... I was thinking before I was brought out of my thoughts by Boogie saying we were here.

Gotti parked the van at the pump and I got out and went inside of the gas station and talked to Hussa behind the counter. I handed him $2,000 and he went and turned the tapes off and I waited in the store. Three minutes later I saw Frank's white Benz pulling in followed by a U-Haul truck. Frank was in the car with two more Cubans and two were driving the U-Haul. I threw my hands up as Frank parked his car on the other side of the pump and the U-Haul parked behind Frank's car. Then I walked over to the van on the front passenger's side window and told Gotti and Tay Boogie let's rock and roll.

I climbed in the back seat of the van and all three of us jumped out the side door holding Draco. Tay Boogie and I ran to the Benz at the same time, Frank was turned around talking to the Cubans in the back seat, he must've seen us because of how big his eyes got. He turned around and Tay Boogie and I let the Dracos go at the same time chopping the Benz into pieces. Then I heard Gotti letting his Draco cut through the U-Haul window. I ran and jumped in the van and Gotti jumped in the U-Haul and threw the dead Cuban out the truck and pulled off. Tay-Boogie walked around putting a bullet in all four of the dead Cubans. When he jumped back in the van I pulled off slowly trying to catch up with the U-Haul, the whole time thinking I hope the work was in the U-Haul.

*   *   *

- *MJ* -

I didn't go to the club and went home instead. Red and Chunky went to the club and when I woke up they both were in the bed sleeping. I went in the front room and there was a bag by the door, I grabbed the bag and opened it and it was the ten bricks, Pops had been here this morning and it was only 8:00am. I wonder what time he came though? I was opening the refrigerator when I heard a phone ringing on the counter, so I answered it and it was a collect call from Tony.

"Princess, why haven't you been answering your phone?"

"Wait, this not Princess but I'll go grab her for you," I said before he cut me off.

"Who is this?"

"My name MJ homie what's up?"

"Princess been dodging my calls, but she has something that belong to me and I need it A.S.A.P and I'm not a nigga to be fuck..."

"Wait, wait, wait Tony before you fuck up. I know some of what's going on, but please save the threats. They're not necessary because they won't work. Now that we got that understanding, I'll do what I can. If I do get it, what do you want me to do?"

"Call this number it's my lawyer, give it to him. Before I hang up, thanks MJ, I won't forget this," Tony said before hanging up.

I threw on the clothes that I had on last night and walked out the door trying to find a restaurant. Every block I walked down I saw hotels and most of all, bellhops and valets. Every other building was bell hop or valet, so I stopped to talk with a black valet.

"Bro, if I wanted to be a valet or bellhop where do I apply?" I asked trying to fill him out.

"Human services, inside," he said pulling out his cigarettes.

"Do y'all got some kind of union?" I asked.

"Naw, but we all eat and talk at the restaurant called Sandys."

"If there was to be a strike who would rally up the troops?" I asked going in my pockets pulling out a fifty and then handing it to him.

"His name is Andre, he's an older skinny man with dark skin. He works at the expensive condos across the street from the club the 'Hot Spot.' You can't miss it," he said taking the money.

49

I turned around and started walking towards the hotel I was staying in forgetting about the food. As I got to the building I instantly saw Andre as he was standing in front of the building. As I walked up he spoke and turned to open the door.

"Hi, Mr. Jones," he said.

"Andre could I have a minute of your time in private?" I asked looking around.

"Sure, what seems to be the problem Mr. Jones?"

"Could you please come up to my apartment?"

"Sure, lead the way," he pulled the door open and stepped to the side. We didn't speak on the elevator and when the door opened, Chunky was in the kitchen naked, she turned around to see who was coming in the door until I called her name. When she turned around and seen Andre she ran in the room, I pointed Andre in the direction of the front room and told Andre to have a seat. Once he sat I turned to him,

"Andre, I am going to be straight forward with you, I need your help and I need this to stay between us."

"You need my help with what?" Andre asked.

"Look, I've come across some drugs and I need help getting rid of them without my father finding out."

"What type of drugs?" He asked not taking his eye off of me.

"Some cocaine."

"Why do you think I could help you?"

"Because you know all the bellhops and the valet, and most of the cab drivers," I explained.

"And what's in this for me?" he said.

"$20,000 a month, $10,000 up front and ten at the end of the month no matter what, plus bonus," I offered him.

"And how does this plan of yours supposed to work?" Andre asked.

I broke everything down to him, "The bellhops and valets would get the work and sell to the tourist and regular residents. The bellhops and valets would get paid off of what they sold. Your job is to find the bellhops and valets who were willing to work," I said looking him in the eye.

"Let me make some calls around and I'll get back to you in an hour."

We exchanged numbers and Andre left with an extra pep in his step. I went in the room and Chunky was in the shower and Red was on the bed sleeping. I walked over to the dresser and grabbed the weed and seen the three x-pills that we bought the other night. I grabbed a pack of blunts and walked back in the front room. Five minutes later, Chunky came out of the shower dressed in a robe, she grabs her phone and came over to where I was.

"Look Chunky, how much of Tony's money did you spend?" I asked hitting the blunt.

"I don't know… around $3,000," she said looking down.

"Well, this is what's going on, Tony called and he needs his money, so I am going to give you the $3,000 and you're going to take it to his lawyer. So, go get dressed so we can get this out of the way… and hurry up," I said.

Fifteen minutes later, Chunky came back out in a Versace summer dress and some flat Versace shoes. I grabbed the bookbag and called down to Andre to have the truck ready. We went downstairs and jumped in the truck and shot straight to Chunky's house. I pulled in the parking lot, she got out, ran upstairs, and came back down carrying two bags.

"Dope Boy told me to give this to you," she said, taking some money out of one of the bags. We sat in the parking lot and counted out $56,000.

"Where is he?" I asked.

"He's on his way down," she said putting her bags in the back seat. Dope boy came down with a garbage bag in one hand, and a bookbag in the other. Then he came over to the truck and handed me the bookbag. He kept walking passed me to the garbage can. I took the bricks out the secret slot and put them into the bookbag, as he walked back passed I handed the book bag out the window to him. Once again, he kept walking in one motion.

I pulled off and went to Tony's lawyer office. I gave Chunky the three-thousand dollars and called his lawyer to inform him she was on her way up. When Chunky came back down we went to a restaurant where I order smoked tuna and rice, a steak dinner for Red, order some kind of fish and a salad for Chunky. We got the food to go and we went to the crib. I took all the money out the truck and put it in Chunky's bag and got on the elevator. Once inside the crib, we took the food into the room and woke Red up. While we ate I told Red and Chunky that I needed a scale, baggies, and razor blades. As Red got dressed, I was rolling up a blunt when Andre, the head valet called.

"Mr. Jones, I know at least five people that are willing to work and we could trust. People have already been asking about how to find drugs."

"Okay, I'll call your phone in about two hours and have you come up," I said hanging up. Then turned to Red and Chunky, "I need y'all to hurry up and go find that…"

*　　*　　*

- Demar -

Once Gotti pulled the U-Haul on the block, Tay Boogie and I pulled behind the truck and I lifted up the door. Instantly, I smelled the vinegar and knew we had hit the jackpot, it was packed with bricks of heroin. As we took the bricks out and counted them, it came up to 65 bricks, that's when I put the bricks in the trunk of the Bentley and Tay Boogie jumped in the U-Haul.

"You know there's still a body in here?" Tay Boogie asked me starting up the U-Haul.

"So, you mean to tell me this nigga Gotti drove all the way here with a body in the U-Haul?" I asked shaking my head and looking at Gotti.

"So, what you want me to do, kick it out on the street?" he asked looking at Tay Boogie like I was crazy. Gotti grabbed the Draco and jumped in the black 745 to follow Tay Boogie to drop the U-Haul off. I went upstairs to grab the money Dino had left and to make some calls. It was time to put the team together… my team. The first person I called was Corty-P because he had the army. He said he was falling back all together because he thinks the police was watching him for a string of murders. Then I called Flight and he said he was sticking to the cocaine.

Next, I called Nico. He was down with the switch but he was going to do his own thing, he was not about to take sides against Pops. Dino was in, and I already knew Boss Ron would go because of his sons. I left $150,000 for Tay Boogie and Gotti to split, and I grabbed everything else. I shot to the crib up north, I had to be sitting down before I called Pops.

*　　*　　*

- MJ -

Red and Chunky came back and I went right to work. I made nine eight-balls out of each ounce. I broke down a whole brick so I got 324 eight balls. I put seven eight balls in each bag and wrapped it up, 46 packs with seven eight balls in each pack, the worker keeps one eight ball and turn in the $1,500. I have 46 packs which came up to $69,000 off of one brick; once we finished bagging up the work I called Andre up and gave him five packs and $10,000 for his ten upfront.

"Each eight ball is $250, and the worker keep one and turn back in $15,000 to you. Call me when someone finish.

Andre left out the door and my phone started ringing. It was Twin. He wanted to get one of them and I told him I'll meet him in Logan Square in an hour. We agreed to meet on Kedzie and Palmer by the park. I walked in the room and Red was rolling up, "Yeah! Roll up two blunts and let's ride," I said putting the work and the money up.

I called downstairs and told Andre to have the car ready, I grabbed a brick and we left. Once in the truck, the first thing I did was go get the Range Rover that was parked at the other house. Red jumped out the truck and jumped into the Audi and followed me to meet Twin. I pulled up on Kedzie and Palmer and then I parked, while Red parked behind me. I blazed up the blunt and ten minutes later Twin pulled up in a Ford F-150. I gave Chunky the brick and she walked over and got inside the Ford F-150, and she returned carrying a footlocker bag.

I pulled off and Red followed me to a car wash downtown, I got out of the Audi and called Pops while they were washing the Range. "Pop's what's going on, what are you up to?"

"I am about to get my hair cut, just trying to clear my mind, but what's up with you?" he asked.

"Need to talk to you about some things," I said watching Chunky smoking the weed in the truck.

"Well, meet me on Jackson…"

"I know where," I said cutting Pop's off before he could finish and we hung up. I jumped in the truck grabbing the blunt from Chunky, Red open the back door and got in. "Look, they said the Range will not be ready until tomorrow because they got to wash the backseat." I was pulling out the car wash when Shine called.

"Hey, MJ, I need to see you about what we talked about," he said as soon as I answer the phone.

"Okay, can you come downtown to Rock-N-Roll McDonalds in thirty minutes?" I ask passing the weed to Red pulling off.

"Yeah, that's…

"And I am a dollar short," I said cutting him off.

"That's cool, see you in thirty minutes," he said hanging up.

I called Pops, "Pops, I need you to come see me."

"When?" he asked.

"Like in thirty minutes,"

"Okay, I guess my hair cut could wait," he said hanging up.

I pulled off going to the crib, I ran upstairs and grabbed the bag with the bricks in there and came right back down. I drove down the street to the Rock-N-Roll McDonalds and parked the truck. Five minutes later an old white dirty beat up van pulled up and parked next to the truck. Shine called my phone and I got out of the truck and got in the van with the bag. As I stepped inside the van, everything was new; hardwood floor, TV's, scanner, and leather. I couldn't believe it and Shine must have known because he started laughing.

"It's to throw people off, they see the outside and look the other way," he said handing me a bag of money. I started pulling out the rolls of money and running through them.

"You know that's eight bricks in the bag, I already gave you one," I said counting the money.

"Yeah, and that's $238,500," he said passing the work to somebody behind me.

I closed the bag up and stepped out the van, once I got back in the truck I pulled off headed home. When I pulled up the valet said, "your Pops is back from out of town." I grabbed the bag of money and told the girls to go grab something to eat and I went upstairs.

Chapter (8)
- Demar -

I was on the elevator on my way up to the condo on the fifth floor when my phone started ringing.

"What's up Tay-Boogie,"

"Demar you need to hurry up and get over here."

"Where you at?" I asked hurrying up off the elevator and opening my door.

"We're at the trap on Leland," Tay-Boogie said before hanging up.

I went to my wall safe and put the heroin inside, then I grabbed my bullet proof vest and the keys to my black Grand National. I also, grabbed my 45. with the drum and then I was out the door headed to Leland to see what was up.

Once I pulled up on the block, Gotti flagged me down and when I pulled over Tay-Boogie was standing next to Lil Jonny's car. He was one of the shorty's who was hustling with Gotti on the night shift. I got out of the car and walked over to Lil Jonny's car. Lil Jonny was in the car naked with his head was cut off sucking his own dick. Then, there was two niggas in the back seat whose tongue was pulled out through their neck's, and their hands cut off.

"What should we do with them? I didn't want to call the police," Gotti said shaking his head.

"No, push the car down on the Jamaicans' side of town, then call the police," I said looking up and down the block.

"Do you think it was them?" Tay Boogie asked looking at me.

"It had to be, but if it wasn't it should have been, but hurry up and move them bodies because we about to go fuck them Cubans up. The right way," I said walking away......

* * *

- MJ -

I got off the elevator and Pops was standing in the front room with a drink in his hand looking out the window.

55

"Your brother Demar has started a war that will divide us and cost us many lives at the same time," Pops said. Never turning around from the window.

"What did he do?"

"He took something from the Cubans, from some good friends and he did something that can't be undone," Pops said walking towards the bag laying by the table. "Nobody knows about this condo but your sister, so I'm bringing you the work that I have left. Tomorrow is our monthly meeting and it's going to determine how we move from there. But this is two million dollars and fifty bricks. I am supposed to collect three million dollars tomorrow at the meeting and our bill is four million," Pops said walking towards the guest room.

He pushed the back wall in the closest and it popped open, there was a floor safe inside.

"The combination is your mother birthday," Pops said opening the safe. It was packed with money, grenades, and some guns.

"Why me Pops? Why show me all this and you have other sons?" I asked looking at him.

"Because you didn't ask for this, and you didn't grow up with money so you'll respect it. You know the value of money, now go get the bag and all the money you're going to put in here and leave some of that work out," he said. I left the room doing as I was told.

Once I came back with the bags, Pops and I started loading the safe up, I kept five bricks out and $10,000. Pops said we was going to have to go to war, because they were going to attack no matter what. Pop's and I had a drink together and he left saying to be at his house in the a.m. around 9:00, then he got up and left. I called Red's phone and told them to come get me.

* * *

- Demar -

Tay Boogie and Gotti pushed the car to the Jamaican's block and called the police, then jumped in my car and headed for Humboldt Park because that's where the Cubans were. They had restaurants on Wrightwood and Pulaski, and on Drake and Cortland. First, we pulled up on Drake because they were in a big building. They were selling grams of heroin and cocaine. Tay Boogie and Gotti posted up across the street in an alley and waited while I rode down the street in my car. There was a lot of people moving around. I waited on the corner parked until I seen one of the Cubans walking across the street. It was a girl about 17 and I came out of my parking spot doing the dash and ran her over and kept going. It was a Cuban building, and when I looked in my rear-view mirror I saw a lot of people running to the girl in the street.

I went around the block and pulled in the end of the alley where Tay Boogie and Gotti was and turned off the lights. After five minutes of waiting I heard Tay Boogie and Gotti going crazy.

"Let's go now!" Tay Boogie said from behind the garbage cans on Drake. They were watching more and more Cubans crowded around the dead girl in the street.

"Not now, just wait a little while longer there's more people coming," I told Tay Boogie when a black 600 Benz pulled up. Three Cubans jumped out standing over the girl. "Now Tay Boogie, let's rock," I said as both of us jumped out with the Dracos and chopped everybody up.

As we ran toward the crown letting the Dracos spit before anybody knew what was going on, we had already killed all three guys that jumped out of the Benz, along with four other people around them. Two women, two men, and the girl on the ground that had been ran over. She was looking bad so the adults kept the kids away from the crowd. Tay Boogie and I emptied our Dracos and ran to the car down the alley where Demar was and jumped in, reloading up the Dracos.

"Now, we hit the restaurant," Demar said pulling off. We pulled up on the next block over from the restaurant and jumped out with Dracos and went through the gang way and came out in the alley of the restaurant and waited. About thirty minutes later, the back door to the restaurant open and a Cuban came out carrying bags of garbage, I instantly ran up to him and up the Draco to his face.

"Where's everybody?" I asked waiting for his response.

"In the office to the right, and in the front eating," he replied.

I hit him with the butt of the Draco and we went in through the back door. I went to the office, Tay Boogie and Gotti went to the front of the restaurant. Once I heard them start shooting I let loose. It was two old man, one younger man and two females. I chopped them up in the small room and turned around and started shooting at the cooks and dishwasher. We went out the back door and Tay Boogie pulled out the

9mm. from his waistband and shot the Cuban twice in the head and we jumped back in the car and pulled off loading back up the Dracos.

We went back to Leland and I parked my car in a garage and I took a cab home to get some rest because tomorrow I had a busy day. Tomorrow was payday.

Chapter (9)
- MJ -

I woke up at four in the morning. Red and Chunky was lying next to me naked, I had been so focused on getting things going right that I haven't been thinking about fucking. I grabbed a blunt off the night stand and went in the front room thinking about my brother Demar, Pops looked so disappointed. He moved the work and some of his money over here, I wonder how the meeting was going to go tomorrow? I was thinking when Red walked over to where I was.

"Let me hit the blunt," she said reaching for the blunt.

I handed her the blunt and walked over to the bar and poured myself a drink. Pops had a chair that sat in front of the window that looked out over the city. I was about to sit down when Red came over and handed me the blunt. I tried to pass her the drink but she shook her head no and bent down and pulled my boxers.

"Sit down," she said getting on her knees in front of me. I hit the blunt and drink, I smoked the blunt looking over the city as Red deep throated me for an hour straight. Once I nutted, she got up and went in the room without saying another word. I stayed like that until six, then I jumped in the shower and woke up Red and Chunky. We got dressed and were out the door by 6:45am. We went to eat breakfast and I gave them some money and dropped them off at the car wash while I hit the e-way on my way to Pop's house knowing it was a big day.

I pulled up at Pop's house at five minutes to nine, and the guard at the gate let me right through. There weren't any cars out front but when I got ready to step out of the car two pit bulls were on the passenger's side door and two was on the driver's side door. Pops came out the front door and snapped his finger and all four dogs came and stood around him. He waved me over and told me to stop while he let the dog smell me, then we went in the house while the dogs stayed outside.

"Have you eaten yet?"

"Pops I ate, and where is everybody?" I asked looking around the room.

"They're on the way now," Pops said leading the way to the room with the table. When we got in there, Pops grabbed the remote control and pushed play, and across the screen read... *'48 Cubans shot and 16 Cubans dead overnight...'*

I looked at pops who was shaking his head, "he has started,"

"Do you mean Demar, is this his work?" I asked Pops not believing what I was looking at.

"Yes! But most of them were innocent, now he did get some of them but at what cost. We're not savages we don't kill women and kids. You see son, a man who has no conscience, no goodness does not suffer." Then Pop's phone started ringing and he didn't answer it as we started walking to the front door. Flight, Boss Ron and Nico were sitting in their cars, he told the dogs to go to the back and they took off as they stepped out of the cars.

"Why do you have them crazy dogs out?" Flight asked as we were walking in the house. But before we could close the door Dino, Curty-P, and Demar pulled in. Once everybody was in the house we went right to the room with the table and everybody was carrying bags - big bags. Everybody sat down except Demar, Pops pushed rewind on the TV and pushed play.

"What happened Demar? Why go to war with them?" Pops asked Demar, shaking his head.

"Because the goods go to the strong and the weak starve, so that the species can get stronger. When the weak hold the goods the strong are obligated to take them, to propagate strength and eliminate weakness," Demar said looking around.

"So, you want to go to war over what, because you think they are weak? Who else do you think is weak, do you think I am weak also?" Pops asked Demar looking him in his eyes.

"Look Pops, I'm selling heroin, we're selling heroin," Demar said waving around the room. "Who's all in favor of selling heroin put your hand up?" Everyone raised their hand but Flight and Demar smiled, "Pops you been voted out."

"Son always remember this, the nail that stands the tallest get hit first. Be my guest, but I am not going to be a part of that part of the game," Pops said standing up.

"Well, I guess this is it," Demar said looking around, and everybody stood up.

"A fool trust on his own heart, but a wise man listens to his counsel," Pops said before everybody left but me, him, and Flight.

"Now what wise man?" Flight said.

"We stay out the way and let Demar finish what he started, because once someone taste's power it is hard to stop them," Pops said grabbing the bags and putting them on the table.

Flight left and said he was about to go out of town for a couple of weeks and would be ready once he got back. Pops went somewhere in the house and came back with a bag. We grabbed all the bags and went to the garage and put them in the bed of the old Ford F-150 and Pops jumped in the driver seat. He told me to follow him and not to let no cars get behind him no matter what, and then we pulled off.

It took us one hour and thirty minutes to get to a little restaurant on 26th Street and Sawyer. It was old and you had to pull around the back to park. Pops parked the truck and we jumped out and went inside, and an old man walks up to Pops and hugged him.

"Flex, this is my son MJ, and MJ this is my friend Flexs," Pops said as me and Flex shook hands.

"I've been dealing with you since we were kids and this is the first time that I have met your son. Come sit down and let's eat," Flex said leading the way to the back. We walked upstairs and into a house, there was an old lady cooking and kids running around the house playing. Pops walked over and kissed the older lady and we sat down at the table. I looked around the old house in amazement because I knew I had just met the connection Things were about to get real.

*   *   *

- Demar -

After we left Pop's house we went to uncle Boss Ron's house while I filled everybody in on what was going on. Curty-P said the only reason why he was there was because I needed his help. I told everybody that I was going to be on Leland and I was giving everybody six bricks of heroin at $40,000 a piece. One of them was just to get started, so the bill was $200,000.

"What about the war that's going on? You cannot make war and make money," Nico said looking annoyed.

"Don't worry about that, I'll handle that," I said looking around.

"Look, I told you I wanted to get into heroin and I think I need your help moving some of it, but I am doing me. I will not be a part of your game," Curty-P said.

"Look, whoever doesn't want to be a part of this can leave," I said and Nico stood up.

"I think this is a mistake Demar. I love you to death, but I am not down with this heroin and war about drugs," Nico said looking around. "We've all made enough money, I am out." Nico walked out.

"Anybody else?" Once nobody else moved I looked at Boss Ron and Dino. "It's us. Curty-P is doing his own thing, all we have to do is sell grams and get security on our spots and the rest will fall in line by itself," I said.

"When are we going to get the work or do you want some money? Whatever it is let me know because this talking isn't shit," Boss Ron said standing up.

"It will be dropped off tonight or you could pick it up on Leland."

"Well, I'll have someone on their way over there in the next hour," Ron said.

"Naw, give me two." And I walked out.

Later that night I gave Boss Ron six, and Dino eight because three was for him. I gave Curty-P six, and he went his own way. But over the next two weeks it blew up, I started off giving away .2 grams for free for the whole day, then the next day people were lined up because the heroin was so strong I knew I could cut it, but I didn't. I started selling grams for $90, four grams for $300 and the block took off, Tay Boogie had the day shift and Gotti had the night. We had put shooters on the front, middle and end of the block and nobody was able to penetrate the security. Now everything was going so smooth.

Pops always said there's always sunshine before the rain, and there's always rain before the storm. Hopefully, everything will stay smooth. I had to call Pops because I need some cocaine.

*   *   *

- MJ -

After me and Pops had eaten with Felix, he said I was always welcome in his house, with or without Pops and we were family. He shook my hand and gave me a bottle of Patron. We jump back in the F-150 and all the bags were gone but one, Pops took me back to the condo and I grabbed the bag from the back and went upstairs. Once in the guest room I open the bag and it was 50 bricks. I put the work up and was walking in the room where Red and Chunky were when my phone started ringing, it was Bear.

"So, you're not going to face me, you're going to hide forever?"

"Bear look, I am not there anymore I'm in Chicago."

"You made me fall off, I had my work and $10,000 in that car, I lost everything plus my car nigga, you have to pay that."

"Look Bear, make it to Chicago and call this number and I got you on my mom's," I said.

"Is that really on your word MJ?

"Yeah, bro, just come it's all good," I said walking over to the dresser where the weed was.

Nigga, I'm on my way now," Bear said hanging up.

There were some clothes bags on the floor, Red was in the shower and Chunky was getting dressed.

"What y'all get me?" I asked looking through the bags.

"Two Nike jogging suits and two pair of Air Max's," Chunky said coming over and kissing me.

"What's that for?"

"Just saying thank you," Chunky responded. I went in the bathroom and jumped in the shower while Red was on her way out. By the time I got out the shower Red and Chunky was dressed, I put on the Nike jogging suit and Air Max's, then I grabbed the weed and called downstairs to tell Andre to have the Audi ready.

"I was just about to call you, everybody is finished with the work and I'm about to bring your money up."

"Naw, just leave it on the seat in the truck and I'm going to give you a bag with more work in it," I said hanging up and grabbing a food bag off the kitchen counter. I put five jabs in the bag and jumping on the elevator

Once we got downstairs, Andre was waiting next to the car, I handed him the bag and we jumped in the truck. I told Chunky to drive and we went out west on Jackson and Kedzie to the barber shop where Pops used to go. We pulled up and Chunky parked so I could look through the window. There was only one person in the chair. I reached over Chunky and popped the slot and grabbed the 9mm. that was in there, cuffed it and got out of the truck and went in. The old man who had cut my hair was sitting in his chair watching TV and froze when he saw me.

"How's everything going?" I asked.

"Look, I don't want any trouble. I told that boy he was wrong," the barber said.

"Look, I didn't come here to start any trouble but I need some help."

"Whatever I could do to help," he said looking around.

"I got some work and I need help moving it." His eyes lit up.

"What you got?" he asked.

"Some bricks for $30,000, whatever you sell them for is on you," I said holding my 9mm. in my pocket of my jogging pants.

"I know some people that be coming around asking,"

"Okay, I'll drop you some off tomorrow, and by the way, where is that lil nigga at anyways?"

"He's in the county jail for an armed robbery, that lil nigga need help. I'm surprised nobody hasn't killed his lil ass out here robbing people then sleeping in cars."

"What's his name?" I asked.

"Luis Smith, but everybody calls him Gimmy That's because that's all he says."

"Okay, I'll be to holla at you tomorrow so be ready," I said walking out to the truck. Chunky drove to the county jail and once we pulled up I gave Chunky the $7,500 that Andre had just left on the seat. I gave her his name and told her to go pay his bond and call me to let me know how much it is before she paid it. Chunky jumped out and went in the county jail to pay Luis Smith bond, she called twenty minutes later and said his bond was $4500. So, I told her to pay his bond, it took her twenty minutes to pay the bond and they said it would take two hours before he would be released. So, we went to Popeyes and got some food and parked so we could see the door where he should come out.

* * *

- Gimmy That -

'*I* *can't believe that bitch ass nigga Sam called the police on me, that bitch ass nigga ran and left me once I got shot, then he gone call the police because I took fifty fucking dollars. I am killing that bitch whenever I see him…*'

"Luis Smith, pack it up you've been bonded out," the guard said walking away from my door.

64

"Aye guard, aye guard, who did you say?" I stood up yelling through the chuck hole.

"Luis Smith."

Then the door popped, now I knew it wasn't me, but I was going to go as far as they let me. I didn't have shit so, I was at the door waiting to go downstairs. The guard came and got me and walked me downstairs. He had my picture in his hand so it had to be me, Sam probably hit a lick and came and grabbed a nigga. I knew my nigga would come through. It took me an hour to get out and once I walked through that last gate I couldn't believe I was out, but nobody was out there to pick me up. Then a fucking Audi pulled up on me and let down the window and a bad bitch with dreads holler, "Gimmy That, boy come on I don't have all day."

I couldn't believe a bitch that bad bonded me out, I jumped in the front seat and she pulled off, and then I felt a gun to the back of my head and I heard a voice say don't move and I knew it wasn't Sam. I should have known that bitch ass nigga wasn't coming to get me, I am going to kill that bitch ass nigga Sam.

*   *   *

- MJ -

"**L**ook lil homie, if I wanted to do something to you, you'd already be dead. Now relax and turn around," I said as the lil nigga turned around and seen my face.

I don't know if he was scared or shocked but he didn't say anything, just looked at me; then he spoke.

"Damn homie, you already shot me now you bond me out to kill me?"

"Naw, it's not like that shorty, I want you on the team," I said handing him the chicken we had brought from Popeye's. He didn't speak, he just looked at me.

"Look shorty, it's not like that Big homie, nobody never did nothing for me, nobody! Now you're going to tell me, I tried to rob you and you're just going to put me on your team?"

"Red pull over," I said and Red pulled over in a gas station. "Look lil homie, it's people everywhere, my truck is on camera and I am not stupid, so I am not going to shoot you on camera, shorty you could leave right now if you want to, if not stop bull shitting and let's get this money," I said putting my gun away.

"Big homie, I am down and to be real, I don't have nowhere to go."

"Don't worry Gimmy, I'm going to fix all that," I said and Red pulled off.

Chapter (10)
- Bear -

'*I got off the phone with that nigga MJ and he said he was going to pay me back. I've been hiding out from these niggas that fronted me the work, because I don't have their money, no car and this nigga took my gun. I'm about to jump on this train and go to Chicago because one, I don't have a choice, and two I have to try to see if this nigga is keeping it real with me because if I stay here in New York these niggas are going to kill me. Plus, I am killing that bitch nigga MJ.*' Bear thought to himself while getting on the train looking around making sure nobody was following him with a knife as his only weapon and fifty dollars to his name.

* * *

- MJ -

"**G**immy That, where do you want to go shopping?" I asked as Red drove.

"Man, Big homie I like Levi's," he said looking out the window.

"Cool, we'll hit the Levi store," I said as Red started heading in that direction. We were already downtown and it only took ten minutes to get to the Levi store. Once we went inside I told Chunky to grab me a couple outfits and handed her the card Pops had given me, "and let shorty go crazy," I said before taking out my phone and walking away to call Pops.

"Pops, I need a new car, where is the dealership you be going to?" I asked walking out the store.

"I don't go to a dealership, I get all my cars from a Latino guy that fixes cars on Fullerton and Albany," Pops said.

"Okay, cool, tell him I am on my way over," I said hanging up walking back into the store. Gimmy That had grab almost ten outfits, socks, and boxers; and Chunky had grab me three outfits. We left the store and went to the Footlocker down the street and Gimmy That had got two pairs of Air Force Ones and three pairs of Air Maxes and we left.

"Big homie I appreciate this for real, I am going to pay you back watch."

"Look shorty, the way you pay me back is by being loyal, that's all I ask of you," I said patting him on the back and when I did I saw him flinch.

"Big homie my arm still fucked up," he said carrying his bags to the truck. I told Red to drive on Fullerton and Chunky took out a blunt and handed it to me. We smoked and before you knew it we were at the mechanic shop. An old Latino man walked up to us with the name Oscar on his blue shirt.

"You must be MJ?" Oscar asked putting out his dirty hands for me to shake.

"Yeah, and you must be Oscar," I said shaking his hand. He started laughing and looked at his shirt.

"No, my name is Miguel, this was the only shirt clean, but your Pops called and said you needed a car. This is what I have now," Miguel pointed to three cars. An Audi A-8, all black with tinted windows, an all-white Range Rover, and a 2019 Ford F-150.

"Naw, I was looking for a new van like this one," I said seeing a light brown 8 door van with a small satellite on top.

"You have great taste. We just finished that one, it was supposed to be for a Cuban guy but he got killed, and he put a down payment on it. We are waiting to see if his family comes to collect the money back or pay the rest for the van," Miguel said walking towards the van.

"How much was the van?" I asked following Miguel towards the van.

"It was $150,000," he said turning around to look at me.

"Why so much?" I asked.

"Because it's bulletproof, and it has a hemi v-12 inside it. Plus, it has cable, wood grain floors inside, refrigerator, and a slot inside," he said opening the doors to the van.

"Are you sure it would stop a bullet?" I asked already knowing I wanted the van.

"Yes! It's bulletproofed like every car your father owns," he said looking at me like I was crazy.

"Okay, take the money off the card," I said looking at Chunky as a signal to pass the card to Miguel. He started laughing again, shaking his head pushing the card away.

"MJ, it's already paid for," he said walking off.

"I thought you said the van was for someone else?" I asked not understanding.

"It was until you came in. MJ, your sister owns this so all the cars in here are really yours, and the keys are in the van with a full tank of gas," Miguel said walking off shaking his head.

"How do I open the slot?" I asked to his back. He said the same way as all the others and I jumped in the van and then we pulled out of the shop and pulled behind the Audi. I popped the slot and the wood grain floor popped open all the way in the back, it was almost big enough to hold a body. I got out of the van and walked to the Audi, "y'all go in the van, and Red, take this lil nigga to get his hair cut." Gimmy That started grabbing his bags.

"Lil homie it's cool, they'll be here when I come back around in an hour," I said. Red and Gimmy That got out the truck and into the van. I shot to the crib and grabbed $10,000 and the five bricks of cocaine. Andre said that everybody was done again so I gave him all the cocaine that I had bagged up and told him to bring the Range around.

"Look, I need a two-bed hotel room somewhere downtown for a couple of days, and I also need an apartment down here anywhere but this building. Take all the clothes in the truck and put them in whatever hotel room." I handed him the work and pulled off with $20,000 and five bricks in the Range Rover.

Gimmy That was an 18-year-old who looked like he was 30. He had rough skin the color of sand paper, with a nappy FRO. He was about 5'9 and weighed around 140lbs but you could see the fire in his eyes when my phone started ringing.

"MJ, are you in Chicago for real?" Bear asked me sounding unsure.

"Bear, I am here just call me when you get down here," I said.

"I'll be downtown at the train station in one hour," Bear said hanging up. I called Chunky and they were at the barber shop on Jackson, so I drove over there. Gimmy That was sitting in the chair and he was already looking like a different person. I popped the slot in the Range for the fuck of it and it open up, there was a 40. Cal and a Mac-11 in it. I set both on the seat and called Chunky and told her to go sit in the van. I put the Mac-11 in the bag with the work and left $10,000 under the driver seat, I put the 40. Cal on me, got out the Range and then jumped in the van.

I popped the slot and took out everything in the slot except for the two bricks. Once I walked into the barber shop I passed the bag to him when nobody was watching. We left the shop and Gimmy That was looking around like he lost something.

"You okay, lil homie?" I asked watching his eyes.

"Yeah, everything is cool," he said walking towards the van. Red continued to drive and Gimmy That set up front with her while Chunky sat all the way in the back of the van with me. I got to get this lil nigga a gun I was saying to myself when Chunky went inside her purse and pulled out a black .45 Glock.

"When did you get that?"

"It was his gun, he dropped it the day you shot him," she said giving it to me. I told Chunky to go sit up front with Red and I called Gimmy That to the back with me.

"Shorty, I'm depending on you to keep our family safe, do you think you'll be able to do that?"

"Big homie, you've done more for me then my own Pops, nobody ever came and got me out of jail before," Gimmy That said looking down.

"Look, I know that I shot you and that you be robbing people, but I am trusting you and I don't trust many people. Gimmy That, just don't let me down," I said looking him in his eyes.

"Why are you trusting me out of all the people?" he asked with tears in his eyes.

"Because I see myself in you Gimmy That, you are me," I said handing him his .45 Glock. He grabbed the Glock and just looked at it, then he looked me in my eyes for the first time.

"Big homie, I am not going to let you down, watch." He tucked his gun and started daydreaming. Andre called me and said the only hotel he could find was the Drake hotel that had two rooms and the clothes were already in the room, and that the front desk was waiting on us. I said thanks and we shot to the room so Gimmy That can take a shower. Once we pulled up, the valet took the truck and gave us the number to the room, the room was on the tenth floor. When we got off the elevator and went to the room, I opened the door and it looked like a crib, front room, two bedrooms and a balcony.

Gimmy That went into one of the rooms and came out smiling. "This motherfucker is nice!"

"Bro jump in the shower and get dressed because we got to move in like an hour," I said looking around at how nice the room was to myself. I went to the bar and poured myself a drink. Red begin rolling up a blunt and Chunky was putting her hand down Red's stretch pants rubbing on her pussy. Red was moving side to side trying not to drop the weed and Chunky was laughing.

"Bitch stop before you make me drop the weed," Red said trying to sound mad. Chunky took her hand out of Red's pants and started sucking on her fingers. "Bitch stop because you know you're making my pussy wet," Red said walking away from Chunky and coming next to me. Red passed me the blunt and started fixing her stretch pants as Gimmy came out of the room looking like a different person.

Chapter (11)
- Demar -

I had pulled up on the block and a couple of shorties were standing around Tay Boogie, he had gone and bought a 2019 Audi A-8 with some chrome 24-inch rims. Tay Boogie was about to get in his car until he saw me.

"Demar, come ride to the restaurant so I can order something to eat," he said as I was walking up. "Plus, I want you to get into my new whip," he said smiling.

"Fuck it, let's go. Where are you getting something to eat from?" I said opening the passenger door and two of Tay Boogie shorties got in the back.

"I want some jerk chicken tacos," Boogie said starting up the car heading to the jerk joint on Broadway and Leland. We all jumped out when we arrived and Tay Boogie was the first one through the door. Once we got inside Tay Boogie ordered 40 jerk chicken tacos for the whole crew. "What you want bro?" he asked taking some money out to pay for the tacos.

"I'm cool, I'll eat a couple of those," I said turning around as I heard a door open to the restaurant. Three Jamaicans walked in, one was tall with long dreads smoking a blunt, the other two was skinny with long dreads.

"Hey fuck boy, why did you leave the car on our block?" he asked looking at Tay Boogie.

"How long is that going to be?" Tay asked the lady behind the counter.

"Around thirty-minutes," she said while Tay Boogie was putting the money back in his pockets.

"Fuck boy, why you do that?" the tall Jamaican asked again as Tay Boogie started walking towards the door.

"Come on bro, let's ride," Tay Boogie said as one of the Jamaicans put his hand on Tay Boogie's chest trying to stop him from moving forward. But one of Tay Boogie shorty stole on the Jamaican that had his hand on Tay Boogie's chest. One of the other Jamaicans upped a gun but Tay Boogie's other shorty grabbed it and the gun went off shooting shorty in the leg. He still didn't let go of the gun, then out of nowhere Tay Boogie upped his gun and shot in the air and everybody stopped. Tay Boogie shorties took the guns off the Jamaicans and made them sit down, Tay Boogie grabbed the blunt from off the floor that the big Jamaican had dropped and started smoking it talking to the lady.

"I'm sorry about that but could you please hurry up with our order?" I had pulled out my gun in the confrontation and now I was putting it back looking at Tay Boogie coughing on the blunt. "Damn dread head, this is some fire," Tay Boogie said with tears coming out of his eyes from coughing. "J-J search these niggas and see if they got some weed on them," Tay Boogie said walking up to the counter to grab the food. "Thank, you ma," Boogie said as J-J searched all three dread heads wiping the blood from his mouth that was running down his chin. Holding the gun in the same hand, J-J found about an ounce of weed on one of the skinny Jamaicans and handed it to Tay Boogie.

Then J-J turned back to the Jamaican that had the weed, "you knew you had the fucking weed on you the whole time and you heard me asking. I should pop your bitch ass," J-J said wiping the blood from his mouth again and slapping the skinny one across the head with his gun.

Boogie pulled out $150 dollars and sat it on the big Jamaican's lap, "this is for the weed," and we walked out the restaurant on our way back to the block.

"You getting some money now you getting soft." I told Tay Boogie getting in the front seat.

"Naw, bro it isn't that, believe me. I am killing them niggas tonight, I just didn't want to do it in the restaurant. And I'm burning that restaurant down because somebody had to call them because I just got this car this morning, nobody knows it yet," Boogie said looking through the rear-view mirror.

"Yeah, you right," I said reaching for the blunt he took.

"And I'm taking this car back I don't want it now."

"Damn, that's fucked up because it's you," I said coughing on the blunt. "Man, this shit is some heat," I said passing the weed to the back thinking about Nico and Pops. This is not how it was supposed to be, I was thinking looking out the window as we pulled up on the block. People were coming from everywhere. "I hope that's not the police watching us in that cable truck," I said out loud but to nobody.

"Shit! I am more worried about the Cubans and the Jamaicans then the police to be honest. It can't be the Cubans because you know they all is in the graveyard," Boogie said passing me back the weed. We jumped out the car and put the tacos on the hood of the car and the whole crew came and grabbed a couple and went back to getting money.

* * *

- MJ -

We got in the van and drove ten minutes downtown to the train station, when we parked I told Red, Chunky, and Gimmy That everything about me and Bear leaving nothing out.

"Why are we here?" Gimmy That asked looking back at me from the front seat.

"Because he's a good nigga. And plus, I owe him," I said looking at Gimmy That. Chunky's phone started ringing from her purse, she was sitting right next to me, she grabbed it out her purse and once she saw the number she handed it to me. I answered it and it was Tony. "Yeah, what's up?" I asked stepping out of the van.

"MJ, this Tony and I was just calling to thank you because most niggas wouldn't have done what you did, but I hope we could link when I come home."

"Don't worry about that, just be cool and hit this number and we'll see what happens," I said watching the people coming out the train station.

"Cool, I'll hit you up when I touch."

Tony hung up and I got back in the van. I was looking out the window and I spotted Bear walking out. He didn't have any bags and he had lost some weight. Bear had on some polo shorts and a pair of Tim's, I seen him reach in his pocket and take out his phone and my phone started ringing, before he could say anything I said, "I'm in the brown van across the street," and hung the phone up. I saw Bear walking across the street and I stepped out of the van, "What's up Bear?"

"What's up MJ, do you have my money?" he asked looking around.

"Bear I got your money, but I am trying to get you to stay down here and fuck with me. A lot has changed," I said moving towards the van.

"Bro, I am cool. I just came to get my money," Bear said as I walked to the van and got in.

"Come on, I'm about to take you to get your money." Bear got in the van also. He was looking scared and when I turned around Gimmy That had upped his gun on Bear from the front seat.

"Man Bear, no disrespect, but you have to get searched, Red search him," Gimmy That said as Red looked over at me. I nodded my head so nobody could see but Red, and she got from behind the driver's seat and searched Bear. Bear only had a knife on him and Red handed it to Gimmy That.

"Turn around, go to the barbershop," and Red pulled off.

"This is how you going to do me MJ? I fucked with you for three years."

"I know and I am going to make it right," I said as Red drove through traffic. We drove in silence, it took us twenty minutes and Red was pulling up behind the Range parking the van. "Bear, step out," I said as Bear stepped out. I stepped out behind him, "Bro, I know what happen was fucked up, but I am making it right," I said handing Bear keys to the Range. "It's $10,000 under the seat, now we're cool right?" I asked looking at Bear.

He jumped in the Range and went under the seat, "Yeah, we cool," Bear said turning off the truck. "Bro why you had to rob me?" Bear asked looking me in my eyes.

"Because Bear, I needed the money and you wouldn't let me work, and you would not have given it to me if I asked. So, I did what I thought was best for me," I said looking at Bear in his eyes.

"MJ, to be real, I don't even have a place to go, them niggas in New York are going to kill me if they catch me," Bear said looking around.

"Bear, can I trust you? Because if you are trying to make some money or need some money let me know. I don't have much after the truck, but for real I'll give you what I can."

"MJ, I wanted to kill you, I even told myself I was going to kill you, but you one of the realest niggas I met bro, I just want to make some money."

"Look, there's money to make, but you're going to have to follow me this time. Bear, we're a family and we move like family and trust. Trust is everything and we're too deep in the game to be sending threats and playing games. Bear please understand, this shit is for real, if this not what you want here's your chance to leave and be safe," I said looking Bear in his eyes.

"MJ you can trust me."

"Well, grab your money and jump in the van so we could hit the clothing store before it closes because we are hitting the club tonight.

*   *   *

- *Pops* -

"**M**elly, what the fuck is going on out there?" The voice on the other end of the phone asked as I sat in my chair.

"I don't understand what you're talking about."

"I told you to stay away from the heroin and you'll be okay, but now you're on the radar."

"But I am not selling heroin, I am sticking to the plan."

"Then you go to war with the Cubans and about to go to war with the Jamaicans?"

"I told you already I am not."

"I know it's Demar, but can't you stop him?"

"No, the family has broken up. It's not the same."

"Well, leave. Get out of there and don't use your phone. Tell everybody to shut down and take a trip. Go see Tasha, go spend some time with her. I am going to make the call, use a new phone and don't say your name just tell everybody to shut down."

"Okay, and before I forget, I found out I got another 26 years old son," I said and the phone went silent.

"Yeah, I heard you. Go see Tasha and I'll get in touch with you later. Ditch that phone."

And he was gone just like that. I jumped out of my chair, I grabbed the million dollars I kept for travel money and jumped in my Ford F-150 and was out the door. I went to the first Walgreens I saw and brought two prepaid phones and called my brother Boss Ron, "Ron, the police are on y'all, the heroin has made y'all hot, shut down now," I said and hung up the phone and threw it away.

Then I called MJ, "Son, the police are on your brother and uncles. The heroin has made them hot, but they don't know you, so stay away from them and be safe. I'll get in touch later because I am going out of town. You already know how to get what you need." I hung up and threw that phone away too.

It was time to go under, once I got to the city I pulled downtown and went into a parking garage and jumped into an all-white Honda that I kept there for just this occasion. I wanted to call Demar so badly but I don't know who's listening to his phone. I knew fucking with heroin was going to bring the heat, hopefully MJ listen to what I tell him and be smart I thought pulling out of the parking garage headed for Mississippi. Tasha had a ranch down there that was off the grid, it was time to relocate and lay low.

Chapter (12)
- Boss Ron -

*...**B**oss Ron was a fifty-year-old gangster and have been getting money and killing niggas with his brothers for thirty-five years without ever being stopped by the police. Now greed had him selling heroin, something they vow to never do...*

I know Melly was going to go underground and I know Demar and Dino wasn't going to go nowhere. So, the best thing for me to do is grab my boys and go underground as well. I got caught daydreaming at the light while I was driving, Melly called me talking about we were hot. I couldn't believe it, I had to keep saying it to myself so it could stick. I could believe myself.

After coming out of my day dream, I shot right to the house and started packing some things. I called my boys, Jermaine and Donnie, and told them to come to the house. Then I grabbed the two bricks of heroin that I had left and the million dollars that Melly kept talking about on a day that we were going to need it but never did. I think things were going to go down this way, I was thinking when Donnie and Jermaine came walking through the door.

"What's up Pops?" Donnie asked looking me in my eyes.

"Look, I need y'all to grab some of the things that you need because we are going to have to leave town for a couple of weeks," I said walking around the house making sure that the windows and doors were locked.

"Pops what's going on?" Donnie asked again eyes bucked looking at his brother.

"Look, you both know I am not going to bull shit or cut any corner with you guys. The police might be on us because of the heroin so before things get any worse we're going to go down south. So, throw away those phones and don't tell nobody where we are going. I have to make a run so be ready to go in thirty minutes," I said standing up grabbing the bag with the two bricks inside and walking out the door.

First thing I did once I got to the car was drive to the train station and put the two bricks inside a box and grabbed the key. Then I went to Walmart and bought four phones and went back to the house. I pulled into the garage and when I walked in the house Jermaine walked straight up to me.

"Pops, what about my truck?"

"Boy fuck that truck," I said walking pass Jermaine and going into the front room. "Look I want both of you to grab a phone out of the bag on the counter and program the numbers you need in them because everybody has to throw their phone away," I said wondering how everything went to shit. Nico had gone off and did his own thing, flight was with Pops, Curty-P was doing his own thing so the only people that really was on the hot list was me, my boys, Dino, and that wild as nigga Demar.

Then I heard Donnie talking about he was ready, so I grabbed my bags and we went through the kitchen into the garage and we put all our bags in the truck and we got into the blue Dodge Charger with tint. I pulled out of the garage and drove straight to the parking garage downtown and switched cars. I parked the Charger there and we jumped in the eight-door van that was registered in this lady Tonya's name who I was dealing with from time to time. I pulled out of the parking garage and I called Demar.

"What's up nephew, I'm calling to let you know to slow down because the spot is hot. Look that heroin has put us on the radar so I am just calling to let you know I am gone," I said hanging up and turned up the radio to head to Mississippi.

*   *   *

- Demar -

It was 7:30pm and I was at my dip crib smoking. Tracey was 25 years old and she was black and Cuban, she was 5'7, 165 pounds, and all ass and titties. Tracey was fixing something to eat when my phone started ringing. It was Boss Ron talking about the spot being hot and he was leaving town. So, once he hung up I called Pops phone but it said his phone was disconnected. Now my mind was wondering if the block was really hot and were the police really watching us? So, I instantly called Tay Boogie and told him to shut down the block and meet me at the club tonight at the Hot Spot tonight at 10:00pm.

Then I called Dino and told him what was going on and to meet me at the club. He said he wasn't going anywhere near the club and he hung up his phone. So, I instantly started thinking could this be my fault? Could I have fucked everything up or is it that nigga MJ? Everything has been okay until this nigga came around, I think I am going to have to drive on this nigga and see what's up. So, I grabbed my bullet proof vest and grabbed my .40 Cal and took my time driving to the club. I had to talk to my crew.

*   *   *

- MJ -

Red, Gimmy That, Chunky, Bear and I went to the clothing store Tops and Bottoms. I bought a white linen Gucci pants suit with short sleeves and a pair of white Gucci shoes. Red and Chunky both got the same all white sheer bodysuit with a white pair of thigh high Jimmy Choo red bottom boots. Gimmy That grabbed a white Prada suit and a pair of white Prada shoes, Bear grabbed a Lacoste suit with a pair of Timberlands. After we finished shopping I dropped Bear and Gimmy That off at their hotel and Red, and Chunky and I shot to the crib and got dressed.

I put on my bullet proof vest and grabbed my van keys and we were out the door. We went and picked up Bear and Gimmy That. We took Bear to the Range Rover and Gimmy That jumped in the truck and they followed us to the club. Before I had valet park the van I popped the hidden compartment and grabbed my .9mm, and when we were walking towards the door the bouncer started approaching me clearing the way. Before anyone of the bouncers tried to search any one of us I handed one of the bouncers $500 and told them we were all together. We got in the club someone instantly took us to VIP.

Chunky and Red hit the dance floor and in their sheer bodysuit you could see both of their pussy and titties like they didn't have anything on. Chunky and Red were dancing on each other and they had everybody's attention. Some bad white bitch had brought two bottles of Remy to VIP for us. Bear was all over her trying to shoot his shot, but she shot him down. While Gimmy That and I were laughing at Bear, I seen some big niggas with long ass dreads walk up to Chunky and slapped her on her ass. When she turned around some words were exchanged then hugs.

Chunky turned and looked at me and then they both started heading my way. "Bae this is Tony," Chunky said walking away.

"Tony what's up, how's everything going for you?" I asked standing up and putting my hand out for Tony to shake it.

"What's up my friend, everything good," Tony said shaking my hand. Tony also was in the VIP and there were about ten other niggas with him. While Tony and I was talking about putting a plan together to get some money, I seen Tony niggas whispering and pointing to some niggas that came through the door. They called Tony over to where they were and when I turned around to look at who they were pointing at I was surprised to see them pointing at Demar and some of his niggas. They were sitting at the bar watching us and smiling. Demar stood up and started walking our way.

*   *   *

- Demar -

We walked in the club and it was packed. We went to the bar and Tay Boogie and Gotti both said that the Jamaicans that we were into it with were in VIP. When I looked over to VIP the first person I saw was MJ. So, I stood up and told Tay Boogie and Gotti to follow me and we headed to VIP with Tay Boogie and Gotti on my heels.

*   *   *

- MJ -

I was looking at Demar as he came toward me smiling with two niggas following behind him, "Bro what's going on?" I asked Demanr with my arm open attempting to show love. But Demar wasn't paying me any attention because he was too focused on Tony and his crew.

"So, this nigga your homie?" Demar asked pointing at Tony and never looking my way. One of Demar's shorties and one of Tony's nigga started arguing, and before anybody could say anything Demar shorty Tay Boogie stole on one of Tony niggas and all hell broke loose. Everybody started swinging, Demar had got knocked down and one of Tony niggas was trying to stomp Demar but before he could I upped my gun and slapped him across his head. Once everybody saw the gun they stopped moving.

"Tony, I don't know what this is about but get your niggas under control so we can talk this out!" I said looking at Tony. But while I was talking to Tony, Demar walked up to one of Tony niggas and stole on him. "Bro slow that shit down you see I am trying to squash this shit and you're trying to keep this shit going," I said pushing Demar away from the nigga he stole on.

"So, this fuck boy is your brother?" Tony asked me looking at Demar then me.

"Yeah Tony, why is it a problem?" I asked putting my gun up.

"Naw, it's cool rude boy," Tony said turning around and walking away.

"Demar what the fuck is going on?" I asked him walking in his face.

"Boy you better sit the fuck down! And the problem is you, you fucking with them clowns. But I am warning you now, don't get caught fucking with them niggas again," Demar said while his two shorties started surrounding me. Then Gimmy That walked and stood beside me, and when he did that I turned and seen Bear out the corner of my eyes turn around acting like he wasn't watching. I told Demar okay and then I made a mental note to watch Bear.

"Bro let's have a drink," I said to Demar pointing to the fifth of Remy that was sitting on the table.

"Fuck it, why not," Demar said walking towards the table. Everybody left me and Demar alone and I instantly addressed what was going on with him and these niggas. "Nothing is going on with them niggas, we've been at war for a minute. What's up with you and them niggas, how long have you been fucking with them?" Demar asked me sipping his drink.

"Bro I wasn't fucking with them like that, but bro you need to slow down for real because Pops said the police was on you."

"Well, if they're on me it's already too late."

"Bro it's never too late, just fall back from selling that heroin for a minute and let me put a plan together," I said watching Bear whispering in Red's ear. Red was trying to move away from Bear but he was grabbing her around her waist.

"Okay MJ, I'm going to listen to you for now because I do believe the police are on me. But let me give you a word of advice, watch the

82

Jamaicans," Demar said standing up and walking out of VIP. I walked over to where Red and Bear were and once he noticed me Bear instantly got up and walked away.

Red walked up to me and said, "bae don't trust that nigga, something up with him. He talking about fuck with him."

"Bae act like you like the nigga and find out his move," I said rubbing Red's ass.

Chapter (13)
- MJ -

That next morning, I started putting things in motion and called Demar. "Bro I need to talk to you and I don't want to do it over the phone."

"We'll meet me at Bally's gym downtown in one hour."

"Wait, I need you to bring me something to eat and the books you were going to give me."

"Boy what are you talking about?" Demar asked sounding confused.

"Bro I need them books," I said saying books louder than the rest of the words.

"Oh, okay, I got you, but make sure you be on time," Demar said before hanging up.

I went in the room and woke Red and Chunky up. "Look Chunky, go get in the shower and get dressed because I need you to ride with me. And Red, I want you to take the Audi truck and go kick it with Bear and remember what I said last night," I said as Chunky got up and went into the bathroom. After Chunky left the room I told Red my plan and she got up and went to jump in the shower. I put on my bullet proof vest and grabbed my gun. When Chunky finished getting dressed we were out the door.

Since we were already downtown it didn't take long getting to the gym. I pulled up in the van and sat in the parking lot with Chunky just looking around. After watching the parking lot for about ten minutes, I told Chunky to give me ten minutes and come into the gym behind me. I got out of the van and walked into the gym and people were everywhere. I walked around the gym until I saw Demar on the weight bench.

"Bro I thought you were against selling heroin," Demar said as soon as he saw me walking up.

"Bro it's not that, but you're going to have to trust me. Plus, the police might really be on to you. Bro just stay off the block and please no selling drugs," I said looking around to see if anybody was trying to listen to our conversation.

"Look MJ, I'm not about to be hiding out from no police," Demar said.

"I am not telling you to hide out. What I'm telling you is no drug selling. Just look at things as if you're always being watched. I got to go but where the work?" I asked Demar looking around for Chunky.

"Bro it's in the black Gucci bag, and just to let you know I want my $90,000 for them two bricks, and please bring my money back in the same black bag," Demar said putting his attention back on lifting weights. I grabbed the black bag and started walking towards the door. Once I saw Chunky I handed her the bag and said let's go. As soon as we got in the van I put the work in the slot and we were on our way back to the crib. As soon as we walked in the house Dope Boy called me and said he wanted two bricks, so I put the heroin up Demar gave me and grabbed the cocaine and shot right back out the door.

*   *   *

- Red -

MJ had told me to act like I was feeling this nigga Bear, so after I got out the shower I put on my yellow summer dress with no panties or bra, the dress was loose and short. So short that if I bend over my whole ass would be hanging out. I jumped in the Audi and drove to the hotel where Bear and Gimmy That was staying. Once I made it to the hotel I valet parked the truck and jumped on the elevator. I got off the elevator wondering how I was going to play this; I made it to the room and knocked on the door. Bear answered in a tank top and some boxers.

"Boy do you got some weed in here?" I asked walking pass Bear.

"Yeah, it's some on the table in a sandwich bag," Bear said pointing at the table. I went to the table and grabbed the weed and the blunt.

"Where Gimmy That?" I asked Bear walking toward the couch.

"He got his ass in there sleep," Bear said sitting on the chair across from me.

I started breaking the blunt down. "Go wake Gimmy That up and see if he wants to smoke," I said laying the weed on the floor and walking to the bathroom to dump the blunt.

"Naw, he cool, let that nigga sleep," Bear said never taking his eye off me as I walked back from the bathroom. As I was walking back towards the couch I kicked the weed that was on the floor everywhere on purpose, then I said damn loud enough to get his attention.

"What happened?" Bear asked me.

"Shit, I just kicked over the weed," I said bending over and picking up the weed. I knew my ass was all in his face and I knew he was looking.

"Damn, that ass everywhere," Bear said from behind me.

"Damn, I'm sorry boy, come pick this weed up for me," I said standing up and pulling my dress down like I was embarrassed.

"Look Red baby, what are you doing with that nigga MJ? That nigga not no boss, he was just working for me, then he stole my money and ran up here. You see he gave me the new Range Rover, he knows what's up. As soon as I find my way I'll be back down," Bear said grabbing the weed from me and rolling up.

"Bear I am going to talk to MJ into giving you some heroin and a block to work it on."

"Damn, you have it like that?" Bear asked passing me the blunt.

"Don't trip, you just need to find some workers," I said lighting up the blunt.

"I want some of that pussy, let me know you're down with a nigga for real."

"You got a rubber?" I asked Bear knowing he didn't.

"Naw, but we can go get one," Bear said reaching for the blunt. I passed Bear the weed and pulled his boxers down and started giving him head. He had grabbed my dreads and wrapped them around his hand. It only took five minutes and I was swallowing down his nut.

"Damn, you'll make a nigga kill somebody over you," Bear said passing the blunt.

"Look, I got to go work on this nigga MJ, but I'll have you some work soon," I said standing up and passing Bear the weed. "Bear don't be telling nobody our business, and before I forget, make sure you take that truck out of MJ's name. Now let me go handle my business," I said walking out the door.......

Chapter (14)
- MJ -

After I sold Dope Boy the two bricks, I went back to the house and started bagging up some cocaine for Andre, the valet. I knew this next couple of weeks were going to be busy so I bagged up two bricks. While Chunky and I was bagging up the bricks, Red walked in wearing a little ass yellow dress. "Red come help us bag this shit up, and how did everything go?"

"Well, I told him I knew somebody that had some work and that I would try to get some for him."

"Okay. Well, he could move the work on Leland and Dover, and I got something for you, but just don't let him know it's coming from me." I said standing up and grabbing one of the bricks out of the book bag and handing it to Red.

"Well, I'm going to help you bag the rest of this work up first," Red said sitting down at the table.

"Red, after you take Bear this work, take him up north and show him where he could get down. Then after that, I want you to meet me at the club," I said as we finished bagging up the last of the work.

"Chunky go wash your hands and roll up a blunt," I said cleaning up the table.

"Bae, I have a headache so I'm about to go take a nap," Chunky said standing up holding her head walking towards the room.

"Let me go wash my hands and I'll roll up," Red said walking towards the bathroom that was in the room. After, I finished cleaning up the table and put all the packs in one big bag I went into the bedroom and Red was eating Chunky's pussy. Chunky was laying in the middle of the bed and Red was on her knees between Chunky's legs eating her pussy. I stood there and watched for a minute, then I took my clothes off and climbed in the bed and started rubbing Red's pussy. Red started pushing her pussy back against my hand.

Now I'm starting to hear Chunky moan, and my dick was rock hard from Red pushing her pussy against my hand. Red's pussy juice was all over my hand. I put my dick in Red and she started pushing back against my dick and slurping loudly on Chunky's pussy. I reached my arm around Red's leg and started rubbing on her pearl tongue while I was fucking her doggy style. After 20 minutes of this and Red started shaking and cumming, I pulled out and Red started cumming everywhere, and then she fell face first on Chunky's stomach and went to sleep.

After Red had tapped out, I went in the other room and jumped in the shower; as I got out the shower I heard my phone ringing. I went to grabbed my phone and it was Twin, the nigga Red had introduced me to.

"MJ, I need to get ten dollars from you ASAP."

"Okay, meet me at Rock and Roll McDonalds in thirty-minutes," I said hanging up. I went in the safe and took out ten bricks and put them in a big bookbag. Then, I called downstairs to Andre the valet, and told him to have the van ready and that I had something for him. I grabbed my gun and put on my bullet proof vest. I had on a jogging suit with some Air Maxes, and with the big book bag I was looking like I was going to the gym.

I grabbed the other bag that I had for Andre the valet and walked out the door. I made it downstairs and Andre was waiting next to the van, I handed him the bag with 92 packs inside.

"Everything I owe you is in the bag in the front seat," Andre said looking around.

"Look Andre, take your $10,000 out of what I just gave you," I said pulling off and calling Gimmy That. "Bro, get dressed and meet me downstairs ASAP."

"Do you want me to wake Bear?"

"Naw, just come downstairs I'm almost there," I said hanging up. Since my condo was down the street from Gimmy That's hotel, it only took me five-minutes to make it to his hotel.

Gimmy That was downstairs waiting, "Big homie what's the plan?" Gimmy That asked when he got in the van.

"I got to bust some moves and I wanted you to watch my back." I was telling Gimmy That as I pulled out of the parking lot on my way to Rock and Roll McDonalds. Once I pulled into the parking lot, I parked the van and kept the engine running. Five-minutes later I saw Twin's van pull in and he parked next to me.

"Gimmy That, make sure you watch these niggas, and if anything goes wrong just start shooting and don't stop," I said grabbing the bag and getting in Twin's van. "Where the money?"

"I see you straight to the point,"

"Yeah, I'm kind of in a rush so what's this?" I asked pointing to the bag that was on the floor.

"That's $285,000; and what's in that bag?" Twin asked.

"It's the ten, and I'm about to bounce," I said headed for the door.

"Okay, I'll be calling you in about a week," Twin said as I was leaving out the van. When I got back into my own van I pulled out of the parking lot watching the mirror to make sure I wasn't being followed. Once I decided I wasn't being followed, I pulled into the first gas station I saw.

"Gimmy That, go in there and get us a pack of blunts," I said parking the van. He got out of the van and I popped the slot in the van to put the money inside and closed it. When he came back getting in the van I handed him the weed telling him to roll up and I pulled off heading to the barber shop to pick the money up from Old School. We pulled up in front of the barber shop and walked in. Old School had someone in his chair and when he saw me and Gimmy That walking in together, Old School stop cutting and started looking at Gimmy That smiling.

"So, Gimmy That, how have you been?" Old School asked looking from Gimmy That to me.

"Old School I've been good, to be honest, I've been really good," Gimmy That said looking around the barber shop.

"MJ, I've been waiting on you. I didn't have your number but give me a minute, let me finish cutting this last head and I'll be right with you," Old School said putting his attention back on cutting hair.

"Look Old School, I need to make a run anyways so I'll be back in thirty-minutes," I said standing up and walking towards the door. We went to Kostner and Cermak to the car auction. "Go in there and look around. Let me make this call and I'll be right in," I told Gimmy That. Gimmy That got out as soon as I pulled in the park lot, and I went into the slot to grab $15,000, and then went into the auction. I started walking around the auction and I see Gimmy That looking at a 2018 all black Impala with light tint, when I walked up on him he was opening the door sitting in the car. "You like that?" I asked Gimmy That.

"Hell, yeah, this motherfucker nice!"

"How much is it?"

"I think $9000," Gimmy That said excitedly.

"Here," I said while going into my pocket counting out the $9000.

"Big homie this for me for real?"

"Yeah, I am going to need you moving around and you're going to need your own car," I said walking towards the front office. It took us thirty-minutes and Gimmy That was following me back to the barber shop. I parked and went inside and nobody was in there.

"Where is Gimmy That?" Old School asked when I walked through the door.

"We just came back from the car lot so he should be pulling up, but grab that for me real quick," I said locking the shop door.

"Come in the back," Old School said and I followed him to the back. Once we went through the door it was a room with a desk, couch and a small refrigerator. Old School opened one of the desks draws and pulled out a bag handing it to me.

"Is this everything for the five?"

"Yeah, everything in there and I need another five soon as you can."

We walked to the front of the shop and Gimmy That was at the door with a smile on his face. Old School walked and opened the door. "Okay, Gimmy That, I see you shining," Old School said stepping to the side so Gimmy That could come in.

"Man, Big homie, I don't know if I said it yet but for real thank you."

"Naw, Gimmy That, thank me with your loyalty," I said handing him $1000. "Now nigga go enjoy your car," I said as we both left the barber shop. I'm heading home and Gimmy That tearing up the street. When I got back to the house I put the money in the safe and went in the room where Chunky and Red was still sleep. I woke up Red and explained the plan to her. She jumped in the shower and I called Demar and made sure he told his shorty on the block what to do.

After Red got out of the shower she put on a tank top and some stretch pants. When she finished getting dressed she grabbed the work and was heading for the door.

"Red met us at the club tonight, at the Red Light."

"Why didn't you tell me that before I got dressed because I can't wear this to the club?" Red said returning to the bedroom and changing into her Fendi body suit and some Fendi Red Bottoms. When she was finished getting dressed for the second time, she grabbed the bag and headed out the door. With Red gone I went into the room with Chunky to take a nap.

Chapter (15)
- Red -

MJ came home and told me what to do. After I got out the shower and got dressed twice, I grabbed the work and went to the hotel where Bear was staying. I valet parked the Audi and went straight to his room. Bear answered the door in a Nike jogging suit and a pair of Air Force Ones. From the look of things, I can tell Bear just got out of the shower.

"So, how did everything go?" Bear asked as I was walking through the door

"Well, MJ don't fuck with heroin so I went to my cousin and got you some work, but Bear, these niggas don't play so please don't play any games," I said going into the bag and handing him the brick of heroin.

"Damn, how much they want for the brick?" Bear asked making a hole in the bag with the truck key.

"$65,000. Plus, we got somewhere to work it," I said walking around the room.

"Where's Gimmy That?" I asked sitting down on the couch.

"I don't know, when I woke up he was gone."

"Well, go check out the block," I said standing walking toward the door.

"Wait, let me get some of that before we leave," Bear said walking up on me and rubbing my pussy.

"Boy, wait and go put that work up so we can go look at the block," I said pushing Bear hand away.

MJ kept telling me not to underestimate Bear, and that he was smarter than he looked. Bear came back from putting the work up and we left the hotel heading to Leland and Dover so I could show Bear where he could move the work. It only took us 20 minutes to reach the block. Once we pulled on the block it was around three shorties and at least 25 hype's walking around looking for work. Bear parked the truck and we got out and walked toward the shorties who was sitting on a stump smoking weed.

Before we could get close up on them one shorty stood up, "man, nothing happening, try back in a couple of days."

"Naw shorty, I'm not trying to buy nothing, I'm trying to sell something," Bear said walking closer to shorty.

"Who are you, nigga? Nigga you might be the police."

"Look, you lil niggas trying to make some money or not?" Bear asked towering over the young boys. They all started looking at each other.

"Shit, I'm down," one said to the other. Then before I knew it and before Bear could say anything else, all three-shorty said at the same time.

"Yeah!"

"Fuck it we down, give us the work."

"Naw, not like that. Where do y'all live?" Bear asked reaching for the blunt one of the shorties was smoking.

"I stay right here on the second floor," one of the shorties said passing Bear the weed.

"My name is Slim," a tall young boy with dreads said.

"My name is Fat Mac."

"And my name is Gunner." Said the one whose house we were in front of. But there was something different about Gunner, he was a pretty boy, a light skin nigga with waves, but he had that look in his eyes that look like death. The look of an old man trapped in a young man body. "What 's your name?" Gunner asked reaching for his blunt.

"Bear."

"So, Bear, where is the work?" Fat Mac aske.

"Look, tell all the customers that tomorrow you will be out here at 6:00am, nothing but fifties and grams for $110," Bear said then exchanged numbers.

We walked back to the truck and as soon as we sat down Bear asked me to direct him to a store to get some baggies, dorms and a blender. So, I told Bear to drive out west, and to pull into MacArthur's Soul Food restaurant. I ordered a fried pork chop dinner with dressing and mac and cheese. Bear ordered a short rib dinner with collard greens and mac and cheese. While we were eating our food, I could see that Bear was deep in thought, "what are you thinking about?" I asked Bear looking in his eyes.

"Shit about to get crazy, I know money is about to come. But I am here by myself."

"MJ is here, he's not going to let anything happen to you."

"Red fuck MJ, once I start getting this money I'm going to do my own thing. Just make sure your cousin keeps the dope coming and don't tell MJ."

"Well, I'm going to the club tonight and MJ is going to be there, are you going?"

"I don't know yet, my mind is on this money," Bear said finishing up his plate. We went across the street to the music shop and Bear got everything he needed, "look, I need a crib around that block, let's go back there," Bear said as we were walking back to the truck. We went on the westside and brought some weed. "So, this the westside of Chicago?" Bear asked looking around.

"Yeah, this is it," I said as he pulled off from the weed spot. Bear was watching everybody and everything, I could tell this nigga was going to be a problem. We drove back to Leland and Bear took down some apartments for rent numbers. After we did that we went back to the hotel. While I was rolling up the weed Bear started bagging up the heroin. I watched everything he did.

He took 50 grams and put it in the blender, then he took six bottles of dorms, broke them down, and put all that in the blender. Next, he took 10 grams of genuine and blended all that up. He poured all that on the table and bagged up $50 bags. Then, he took 25 grams and bagged that all up in grams. He bagged up 320 bags and they were $50 bags. He put 7 bags in a baggie and put it aside, he made 45 packs.

"So, if you give them 7 bags how much do they keep?" I asked.

"They turn in $300 and keep $50."

"So why did you bag up so much?" I asked Bear.

"Because there were so many customers out there I know it's going to sell. Plus, this dope is strong and it's going to draw customers," Bear said cleaning up the table.

"Boy, you been bagging up that shit for three hours, I'm about to go. Are you coming to the club?"

"I don't know. If I decide to go I'll call you."

"Well, I'll be over here to help you get to the block in the morning."

"Naw, I got the address in my phone from the apartments that was for rent. I could pull it up in my navigation, as a matter of fact, what's the name of the club.?"

"The name of the club is the Red Light." I told Bear standing up walking toward the door. "And hopefully, I'll see you at the club…" and I'm thinking this nigga Bear was about to get money.

Chapter (16)
- MJ -

I woke up around 6:00pm, and I was in bed by myself. I was looking around the room for Chunky but she wasn't in there. I got up and started walking around the house. I went in the front room and there she was hanging up the phone. "Go get in the shower because we got to go. Plus, we're going to the club tonight," I said as Chunky got up and started walking towards the shower. I went into the other room and opened the safe, I took out 7 bricks. I was grabbed the weed off the dresser when Red walked through the door. I rolled up the weed and Red went on to tell me that Bear was getting down tomorrow. Bear said he wasn't selling anything but $50 and how he bagged up $13,000 in $50-dollar bags

I knew Bear's grind. I knew Bear was going to get a lot of money and fast. While Red was telling me about Bear, Chunky came out of the room with an all-white lace bodysuit and a pair of white 6inch Red Bottom heels. I passed the blunt to Chunky and I started thinking about everything. *'Why was I helping Demar? I know he is my brother but should I be putting myself on the line?'*

I came out of my daydream. "Come on let's ride," I said standing up. I put on my bullet proof vest and grabbed my gun, then I called downstairs and told them to have the van ready. I grabbed the 7 bricks that I took out and headed out the door. Once we got downstairs to the van I popped the slot and put the 7 bricks up and we drove to the Cheesecake Factory to get something to eat. While we were eating Chunky asked me what club we were going to and I told her the Red Light as we were getting ready to leave the restaurant. Red and Chunky went to the bathroom and I went and pulled the truck around to the front of the restaurant.

"Where is Chunky?" I asked Red as she opened the passenger door.

"She should be coming out because she was washing her hands when I came out," Red said getting in the van and closing the door. We sat in the van for five minutes before Chunky came out of the restaurant and got in the van. Once Chunky got in I got in the back seat and told Red to drive and to go to the barber shop where Old School was. When we got there, I popped the slot and took out five bricks and took them into the barber shop. I talked to Old School for a minute, he was telling me I should start buying buildings, fixing them up, and start turning my money over. Old School gave me something to think about.

We left the barber shop and headed to the club, it was almost 9:30pm and when we pulled up I saw Gimmy That out front posted. It was Friday and the line to get in the club was around the corner. We walked to the front of the club and I gave the bouncer $500 to let me, Red, Chunky, and Gimmy That in the club without being searched. Once we got inside the club we were taken straight to VIP. Red and Chunky were walking around the club while Gimmy That and I were toasting when my phone started ringing. It was Demar asking where I was. When I told him the Red Light he said he was coming so don't leave because he had to talk to me.

Damn, I couldn't stop wondering what it was? About 30-minutes later, Demar came through the door followed by three of his shorties, Tay Boogie, Gotti, and JJ. They were moving through the crowd like an army. Demar came to me and went on to tell me that he was about to go out of town for a couple of months and he wanted to thank me for trying to get the police off his back. Plus, he wanted to give me some heroin before he left because he wasn't going to be here. As we were talking Tony and about 10 Jamaicans walked through the door, Gimmy That caught eye contact with me and nodded his head in the direction of Tony's Crew.

Tay Boogie picked up on what Gimmy That was pointing at and was about to go towards Tony, but Demar stopped him saying he was here to party. I was watching Tony when Chunky walked up to Tony and gave him a hug. Tony and his crew went in VIP right across from us and some of his niggas was mean mugging us but everybody was doing their own thing. Red and Chunky came back to VIP where we were. After about an hour of drinking and smoking weed in VIP Demar said that he was about to leave and that the heroin for me was in his car. So, when Demar got up to leave me and Gimmy That followed him towards the door.

I looked back toward Tony to make sure we weren't being followed, but Tony was on the phone. I started looking around for Chunky and Red but I didn't see them. By the time we were at the door, Tay Boogie and JJ were the first out the door. Once Demar stepped out the door all hell broke loose. Someone was across the street shooting, JJ got hit 9 times with an AK-47, Demar tried to run back in the club but everybody was running out the club because someone was shooting inside the club. Everybody was running towards the door pushing everybody outside. When Demar realized he couldn't run back inside, he tried to duck and run outside behind a car but was shot three times in the chest. The force from the 12 gauge was so strong it pushed Demar into the car splitting his head open knocking him unconscious.

Once the shooting stopped, Gimmy That and Gotti broke out the club shooting. It must have caught the shooter off guard because the one that was shooting the AK-47 took off running toward a car that was parked. But before he could jump in the back seat Gotti and Tay Boogie riddled the shooter with bullets and they kept running. So many people were running out of the club that I got ran over and stomped. Once everything was cleared, JJ was dead, Demar was shot multiple time, plus one of the niggas that shot Demar was dead. I was looking for Red and Chunky but didn't see either one of them.

The police and ambulance came, Demar had a light pulse so they put him in the ambulance and gave him a police escort to the hospital. After I saw them pull off with Demar, I walked over to where the dead shooter was and when I looked down at him he was a Jamaican. I instantly turned around looking for Tony. I didn't see him or any of his niggas so I went to the parking lot looking around and nobody was there. But I did see Demar's Bentley Coupe, I remember he had the work in his car so I busted the window and grabbed the book bag. I saw my van a couple cars away. I made it to the van, got in and popped the slot to put the work up.

I pulled out of the parking lot and the first person I saw was Red and Tay Boogie. When Red saw the van, her and Tay Boogie started walking and got in the van. "Where's Chunky?" I asked Red looking around. Then I saw Chunky walking up the block from the opposite side of the street from the club, Chunky jumped in and we headed to the hospital to see Demar.

Chapter (17)
- Tony -

We went to the Red Light to celebrate, it was my brother's bachelor's party. We were deep and about ten of the rude boys walked through the door of the club and the first person I seen was Princess. Once I seen her, I knew that nigga MJ was here somewhere. When I found him I also found Demar. But they had some nigga with them that wasn't drinking or partying, just watching us. So, I knew it was going to be hard getting to the both of them niggas, I was thinking to myself before Princess walked up to me.

"Tony can I get a hug?"

"Yeah, baby, come here," I said grabbing Princess's ass. I knew MJ was watching me and I was trying to get under his skin, but it was too dark for MJ to see exactly what I was doing, yet he was looking at me. So, I played like I wasn't looking.

The crew and I partied but the whole time I was watching MJ. Around 1:00am MJ and Demar started walking toward the door. I'd already had everything set up, so as soon as MJ and his crew made their way toward the door, MJ turned around and saw me on the phone. Soon as he turned back around I started shooting and the crowd started rushing out the door pushing MJ, and his whole crew out the door. I couldn't see when MJ and his crew made it out the door but I knew because I heard the shots. Some people in the club started to duck under tables and stopped by the front door, but I started shooting again, forcing everybody to stampede towards the front door and forcing MJ and his crew no choice but to go to the front door or get run over.

I knew there was a couple of Jamaicans out front waiting on Demar, MJ, and his crew to walk out the door of the club and get shot to pieces. As I heard the shots in front of the club I waited until the shooting stopped, then my boys and I started walking to the back of the club where I found the back door and we snuck out trying to avoid the police who were driving off following Demar to the hospital. When we were coming out the back door there was a couple of cars coming up the alley, a white blazer and an impala. Knowing MJ didn't drive anything like that made me put my attention back to worrying about the police.

*   *   *

- *Gimmy That* -

We were leaving the club. I was really looking out for MJ, and Gotti was looking out for Demar, because Gotti and I walked out the door first and as soon as we cleared the threshold the shooting started. JJ was killed instantly. Demar was shot multiple times, while MJ and I ducked behind cars in front of the club until the shooting stopped. Before the shooter could make it to his getaway car Gotti and I chased him down for the over kill. The car he was about to get in pulled off and we both tried to chase the car while still shooting. It was useless, and only the back window was shot out.

I had parked down the street from the club and once we stopped chasing the car we were right next to my car. We both got into my Impala, but before I could pull off the police and ambulance pulled up like they were parked around the corner. So, we stayed in the car until the police loaded someone in the ambulance and gave them a police escort away from the club.

"Pull around the block and let's check on Demar," Gotti said looking around in the car. I pulled down the alley trying to hurry up, but there was a white blazer in front of us. When we made it behind the club, Gotti hollered, "there go them fucking Jamaicans right there! Stop!" He was saying as he started rolling down his window, I passed my gun to Gotti and pulled up on the Jamaicans, maybe three feet away and stopped.

*   *   *

- *Tony* -

As we were walking down the alley in a hurry and still worrying about the cops, a black Impala stopped right in front of us. I instantly recognized that it was one of Demar's security from the club, and he had a gun in his hand. Before I knew what happen he started shooting. My brother was shot in the head and chest, and he died before he hit the ground. Then, the nigga with the gun got out the car and started walking toward us shooting. My cousin had run passed the shooter but the driver ran him over. Then we reversed back over him leaving him stuck under the car. I tried to run and was shot in the back up by my shoulder, so I ducked in between two garbage cans. Then I heard the car pulling off.

*   *   *

- *Gotti* -

I told Gimmy That to stop the car and he handed me his gun, he stopped the car at the perfect spot because I jumped out the car and went crazy. The first person I saw I shot in the chest and head killing him instantly. I started shooting anybody I could get close to. Then Gimmy That ran over some nigga, and then reversed back over him and kept the car on top of him while I was still shooting. After I was sure I had killed at least two niggas, I told Gimmy That to pull off and don't speed. Everything had happened so fast. The police must have heard the shooting because as we pulled to the end of the alley the police was running from around the club.

"Where is the shooting coming from?" one of the police asked five feet from the car.

"They're back there shooting... back there!" Gotti said as I pulled off and the police ran to the back of the club looking for the shooter.

Chapter (18)
- MJ -

After I picked Chunky up, I followed the ambulances to the hospital. Tay Boogie and I sat in the van while Chunky and Red went in to see how Demar was doing. We stayed in the van because I didn't want the police asking us questions or connecting Demar with me. I knew Demar was hot. Red called me and said Demar was going into emergency surgery. I told her to stay in the waiting room until she found something out and called me once the police left.

While we were sitting in the parking lot Tay Boogie asked if I had some blunts in the van and he started going through his pockets looking for his weed. I handed Tay Boogie the blunt and he instantly started rolling up, as we were smoking the blunt the ambulances and police started pulling into the hospital emergency room back to back. Five minutes later Chunky called me and said Tony had been shot and his brother, cousin, and two of his homies had been killed. There were also about five of his homies in the waiting area with them.

So, I told Chunky to come get in the van and I called Red phone, "baby look, I told Chunky to come to the van because I didn't want one of them Jamaicans to see her and recognize her. They were too busy worrying about Tony now to really pay attention to her. Plus, if one of them niggas try to holla make sure y'all exchange numbers, and I'll be in the parking lot waiting on you," I said grabbing the blunt from Tay Boogie.

"What's going on, and who was going into the hospital?"

"That was my bitch and she said that like three or four Jamaicans have been killed, and Tony has been shot."

"Look MJ, you're going to have to take Demar out this hospital as soon as possible because if they find out he's here they're going to kill him. Only family can have a patient moved or discharged from a hospital," Tay Boogie said looking concerned.

Chunky came out of the hospital and got in the van. We stayed in the van for another hour before Red called saying Demar was out of surgery. She said the surgery went well but Demar was in a coma. Tay Boogie had me drop him off at his car and he was going to get up with me in the morning. So, I dropped Tay Boogie off out south on the low end to his car and I drove back to the hospital to get Red.

"Where is Demar?"

"He is in intensive care."

"Look Red, just come down to the van and we'll be out here tomorrow," I said starting up the van and pulled up to the emergency entrance. Once Red came down and got in the van she started telling me that one of the Jamaicans came and sat next to her and asked who was she waiting on. She told the Jamaican she was waiting on her grandfather who was in surgery because he had a heart attack. She went on to ask the Jamaican what was his name and he said Wayne. Red asked Wayne what he was doing there and he went on to tell Red how they were coming out the club Red Light and a black Impala pulled up on them and somebody jumped out and started shooting and four people were killed.

Red and Wayne traded numbers and Wayne said he was going to call her in a couple of days. After Red told me what Wayne said I called Gimmy That and he answered on the first ring.

"What's up big homie are you okay?" Gimmy That asked.

"Yeah, I am good, but why didn't you call me?"

"Because I didn't know who was around you, so I was waiting on you to call me," Gimmy That replied.

"Who are you with now?" I asked.

"It's me and Gotti coming from the weed spot out west, what's up?" Gimmy That asked concerned.

"Look, meet me at Old School's barber shop in thirty minutes," I said hanging up. I drove to the house and told Red to get in the Audi and meet me at Old School's barber shop. Red got out of the van and I pulled off headed out west.

It was 4:02am and I wanted to be back in the house before the sun came up. When I pulled up at Old School's shop, Gimmy That and Gotti was sitting in the car smoking weed like nothing had happened. I pulled behind Gimmy That's Impala and hit the horn and Gimmy That and Gotti both got into the van.

"What's up big homie? Do you want to hit this weed?"

"Naw, bro but I want you to get out of that car because it's hot.

"Big homie fuck them, this is all I got."

"Look, don't worry about the car I'm going to get you another car, but until then you could drive the Audi truck," I said reaching for the weed. Red pulled up across the street from us and parked, and then came over to the van and got in; she handed me the key and I handed it to Gimmy That. "Look Gimmy That, give me your gun, and yours to Gotti."

"My gun, why?" Gimmy That asked.

"Because they're hot and if y'all get caught with them guns y'all will never coming home," I said handing Gimmy That my gun and taking both of their guns. "Look, I'm about to head to the crib, but I am going to come pick you up at the hotel when I get up."

"Naw, just call me because I'm about to go with Gotti over some bitches house," Gimmy That said reaching for the door.

"So, what's up with Demar, how is he doing?" Gotti asked.

"He's in a coma, but he is going to be good."

"…And what about Tay Boogie?"

"He's cool, I dropped him off at home out south, but JJ got killed," I said.

"Yeah, I know, but we got them nigga's back," Gotti said slapping hands with Gimmy That.

"Look, y'all be careful and answer your phone because I'll be to get you tomorrow." They got out the van and I went home. I needed some sleep because I had a big day tomorrow.

Chapter (19)
- Bear -

After bagging up the heroin Red gave me, she left. I said I might come to the club, but I had a lot to do. I started calling apartments and I had three interviews lined up to see them, I was thinking as soon as I got up this morning. I was going over everything that happened yesterday in my head when my phone started ringing.

"Bear are you up and on your way?" Gunner asked as soon as I answered the phone.

"Boy, it's only 5:00am, I said at 6:00am, but yeah, I'm on my way," I said before hanging up and getting dressed. I grabbed the work and was out the door. It took me 20-minutes to make it to the block and when I pulled up, all I see Gunner and Slim, and nobody else. So, I parked and gave Gunner the work and got out the truck. "Has anybody showed up yet?" I asked.

"Yeah, they were over in the vacant lot," Gunner said going into his building. I went and looked at the vacant lot, there was a wooden gate up front so I couldn't see inside, but there was a hole in the gate about four feet across, so I walked inside. I was at a loss for breath. There was around ten people that came up to me asking if I had the work.

"Naw, he's on his way now so everybody line up and with your money out in hand."

I was telling Slim and Gunner to come into the vacant lot, "everybody who want grams line up over there, and anybody who wanted $50 bags line right here." It was like a stampede. Customers started coming and going from everywhere, and after five hours Gunner had sold $52,000. I knew right then and there shit was about to get real.

It was 11 am and I had to be at one of the apartment interview's at 11:30am. I told Gunner I'll be back and I jumped in the truck and pulled right around the corner. The apartment was in a two-flat building, I called the landlord and told him I was downstairs. A 60-year-old black man came out. We exchanged names and he showed me the apartment, it was a two-bedroom with two bathrooms on the second floor. I looked around the apartment, but when I looked off the enclosed back porch and saw Gunner and Fat Mac in the vacant lot hustling I knew I wanted it. So, I discussed rent.

He wanted $1500 plus security deposit, so I gave him $3000 and asked him when could I move in? He handed me the keys with no lease or nothing to sign. After I got my keys to the apartment I went to the hotel and grabbed all my things and looked around for Gimmy That, but he wasn't there. It looked like he hadn't been there so I just grabbed my shit and left. I made it back to my new apartment and I didn't have shit in there but a refrigerator and stove. I had $5000 left over from my money that MJ gave me, so after I put the work up I drove until I saw the first furniture store and pulled over.

It was a family owned furniture store and the furniture store was nice looking. It was cheap, but I needed something in my apartment so I got a bed, front room set with two end tables, three couches, coffee table, and two tv's with free delivery for $2,500. I gave them the address to deliver the furniture and went back to the house. I was looking off the back porch and all I saw was customers. I went back to the front of the apartment and started looking out the window because the furniture man said he would be at my apartment with the furniture in two hours.

I went downstairs and sat on the porch and waited, while I was waiting the downstairs neighbor came out smoking a blunt.

"So, you moved upstairs, what's your name?"

"Yeah, and my name is Bear. What's your name?"

"Kesha, and where are you from because you're not from around here, I could tell from your accent.

"I'm not from around here, I'm from New York, but you're not from around here either, where are you from?" Bear shot back.

"I am from Jamaica," Kesha said passing me the weed. Kesha was a caramel skin, long dread stallion, she was 5'7 and weighed 150 pounds all ass and tits. Kesha looked like she was about 25 years old, we sat on the porch, smoked, and talked. I found out Kesha didn't have any kids and she stayed there with her mother and father. She had a brother, but he didn't live with them, she had been in the United States for three years and she didn't have a nigga.

We talked and smoked, and before I knew it the furniture driver was pulling up with the furniture. "Kesha, would you show me where Walmart is after they leave?" I asked her walking up the stairs.

"Yeah, I got you. I'll be on the porch when you ready," she said as I walked up the stairs. It took them 20-minutes to bring the furniture up, after I locked the doors and went downstairs, Kesha was still on the porch. She had on a pair of white stretch pants, white tank top, no bra, and a pair of white flip flops sandals. "Your girl not going to get mad because I am riding in your car, is she?"

"Naw, she isn't going to get mad because I don't have no girl, I live by myself," I said walking off the porch toward the truck.

We went to Walmart and when Kesha got out of the truck her ass was shaking like Jell-O.

"What do you need to get out of here?" Kesha asked me grabbing a shopping cart.

"I need everything because I don't have anything in my house: no towels, sheets, broom, mop, pots nor pans. I need everything," I said grabbing me a cart. We stayed at Walmart for two hours and when we were about to leave, I told Kesha to grab some food for me, "something you could cook because I don't know how to cook," I said smiling at Kesha.

"Boy, nobody about to be cooking for you," Kesha said walking toward the food department.

"...And I like breakfast and jerk food," I said laughing and watching Kesha's ass while she walked away.

Once we got to the counter, everything we got cost $1,324. I pulled the truck up to the door and we put everything in the truck before leaving to the house. Kesha helped me bring everything up, the house was already clean so while I put the blinds up, Kesha put the towel, food, and other things up. Then she made the bed.

"Boy! I should be getting paid for all this work," Kesha said sitting down on the couch and rolling up a blunt. After we smoked, Kesha left and I went out the back door and walked through the gangway right on the block. Fat Mac and Slim were in the vacant lot.

"Where is Gunner?" I asked Slim as customers walked pass.

"He ran in the house, he'll be right back out," Slim said serving a customer. It was almost 6 o'clock pm and things weren't slowing down. I saw Gunner walking out of his building towards me.

"What's up Big Homie?"

"How's things going?" I asked walking toward Gunner.

"Things are good. We did about $10,000 so far, but we'll be through everything tonight." Gunner was saying when an old white hype walked up to us. He was selling two 45's for $400, I gave him the $400 and told him if he had anymore to bring them to me. I kept one of the guns and gave one to Gunner. I told Gunner to go grab the $10,000 and I went to the house to put the money up and to bag up some more work.

I set up shop in the extra room. Out of the 100 grams I was making 30 grams at .09, and out of the rest I bagged up $14,000. I was bagging up $17,000 out of 100 grams. Over the next week my routine was the same: I would go on the block in the morning and watch Gunner, Slim and Fat Mac until around 10:00 o'clock pm, then I would come back and smoke with Kesha. The block was booming so Gunner started recruiting more shorties to work. So, it went from Gunner, Slim and Fat Mac on the block to ten shorties with them on the block. It was time to call Red and get some more work.

*   *   *

- *Gunner* -

This nigga Bear had come and turned the block up with that dope, Fat Mac and Slim started recruiting all the shorties in the neighborhood. It started from the block doing $10,000 to $15,000 to $20,000. Fat Mac and Slim was making $1000 a day easy and I was making $2000. I had gone and bought two ounces of cocaine after the second day and I was selling $50 bags of cocaine, and I had Fat Mac and Slim passing out packs of the cocaine. By the end of the week the block was booming, bitches everywhere, nigga's everywhere.

We got hypes doing security at the beginning of the block watching for police and at the end of the block. It was crazy. We had brought five guns and Bear had rented us a three-bedroom apartment on the block. Somewhere for us to kick it at. Everything was going a little too good, so I knew the storm was coming. It was so many shorties on the block on shift, the older nigga's that was trying to work took the night shift. Fat Mac was running night shift and Slim was running the day shift, and all the hood rats started hanging around because they smelled the cheese.

Chapter (20)
- MJ -

I woke up and Chunky and Red were still in bed. I went in the front room and sat in Pop's chair wondering what he would do now. Demar had been shot up last night and now he was in a coma, but the only thing I could think about was Pop's saying "no matter what, family first." So, with that in mind I knew I had to get Demar out of that hospital.

The first thing I did was find and call a real estate agent. I asked her if she had any fixer uppers, she asked what was my price range and I said $10,000. She said she had some, but they were in really bad shape. So, after telling her I still wanted to see the building we agreed to meet at the building on Fullerton and Albany, in one hour. I jumped in the shower and put on my bullet proof vest. I also put on one of Pop's Tom Ford suits. I grabbed my gun and was going to the safe to grab $10,000 when Shawn called.

He was Pop's customer. I had sold him some work before, but not three. Instead, I grabbed five bricks out the safe and told Shawn I would meet him in two hours. I went and met with the real estate agent whose name was Trinette, she looked like she was around 25 years old, but I could tell she was older. I was already there waiting when Trinette pulled up in a 2010 750i. Trinette got out of the car and showed me the building. It had been in a fire and all the copper was gone out of the building. There were only 9 two flat brick buildings, but the inside was destroyed.

"So, this is $10,000?" I asked Trinette walking around the building.

"No, it's $15,000, and you're not paying for the building you're paying for the neighborhood."

I had watched so many episodes of Flip This House that I had basic understanding on how to flip a house. "Look Trinette, could I give you $9,000 now and the other $6,000 next month?"

"Yeah, that's cool, just bring a check to my office and sign your name to get your keys. Once you sign the contract and you don't pay in 30 days, the building will be taken because it's always all money due at signing on these kinds of buildings."

"Okay. Well, I'll be at your office in 30 minutes." Trinette handed me one of her cards and got in her car. I went to the bank and got a $9000 cashier's check and went to Trinette's office and gave her the check. Signed some papers and got the keys. I sat in front of Trinette's office and called Shawn and told him to meet me at Home Depot.

When I pulled the van inside the parking lot of Home Depot, there were about a hundred Mexicans looking for work. So, I pulled over and about ten Mexicans came running to the van. I parked and walked up to the Mexicans and told them I needed a building fixed that had been burned up. While I was talking to the Mexicans I saw Shawn pull in the parking lot and I told the Mexican that I would be back in 20-minutes to take him to see the building.

I walked to my van and popped the slot and took out three bricks, then I pulled my van next to Shawn's car, Shawn got out and got in the van carrying a book bag. "Do I need to count this?"

"Naw, it's all there." Shawn grabbing the bricks and getting out the van. I put the money in the slot and went to pick up the old Mexican man to take him to the building to see if he could to do the work. Once we made it to the building the old Mexican man whose name was Pablo, got out of the van and looked around the whole building from the inside out without saying a word.

After Pablo finished looking over the building he turned to me and said, "the bones of this building are good but the whole inside is destroyed from a fire. I could fix it, but it's going to cost some money because everything on the inside is going to be replaced." Pablo went on to tell me to fix the house up right could cost $100,000 and it would take 30 days. So, I asked Pablo if he could finish in two weeks and I'll give him a bonus. He said he'll do his best.

I drove Pablo back to Home Depot's parking lot where his work truck was. "So, when do you want me to start?" Pablo asked.

"Look, I need you to start today."

"Well, I'm going to need some material, a couple of spools of copper, wood boards, and whatever type of flooring you want to put down," Pablo said.

"Go in and start getting the things you needed and I'll be right behind you." While Pablo went into the store, I went in the slot and took out $10,000. I went in the store and got all the things he needed. Everything came out to $17,000, but instead of paying cash I paid with Pop's credit card.

After we got all the things Pablo needed we loaded everything on Pablo's truck and drove to where everybody was standing looking for work. Pablo got out his truck and picked five men to help fix the building. He told them they were going to work 10 hours and get paid $10 an hour. I told him to pick a couple more workers so he could speed up the job, but Pablo told me five would be all he needed for now.

I loaded some of the people he selected in my van and he put the rest in his truck and we went to the building. I gave Pablo the keys, we exchanged phone numbers, and I took a picture of his I.D. After, getting Pablo settled, I called Red and told her and Chunky to take the Impala and go to the hospital to check on Demar. Then, I called Gimmy That and asked, "where are you located?"

"Out south with Gotti and Tay Boogie," Gimmy That answered.

"Meet me at the barber shop." And I went to check on Old School. I pulled up and nobody was there but Old School, so I jumped in his chair and got a haircut. Not long after getting my haircut, and talking to Old School, Gimmy That pulled up. All three of them came in and I could tell those three together was a problem for somebody.

Tay Boogie started telling me they had been out south looking for the Jamaicans. He continued on to explain that it's been a war between Tony and Demar, but Tony got locked up and his soldiers went into hiding. "They even stopped working their blocks, but they started working a couple of blocks down from one of Demar blocks," he finished.

"Well, this is what I'm going to do. If y'all trying to work I got some work for y'all, and if y'all trying to go to war I'll get some guns for y'all."

"Look, we're trying to do both, but we need some money."

"Tay Boogie we got money. Don't worry about that," I said getting out of the chair.

"I know there's money around, but if we start knocking off the soldiers then Tony will never come around. We've got to hit him where it hurts. We're going to have to take all his customers first," Tay Boogie said.

So, I walked out the barber shop and went in the van and grabbed the two bricks. I gave them to Tay Boogie and told him that's for all three of them and to give me back $50,000.

I went back to the house and started bagging up some jabs for Andre the valet. I tried to call Bear but he didn't answer. Over the next week everything went along smooth. The building was coming together,

I had gone and got the drywall, paint, tub, counter top, etc. Also I was moving the last of work I had.

Then, Bear called Red and said he needed some more work for him, and somebody else. He wanted to get fronted one again. Plus, he had a customer that wanted a brick of heroin, and a brick of cocaine if her cousin had it. I gave Red two bricks of heroin and one brick of cocaine, then told her she should be coming back with $160,000. "See what's been up with him and find out where that nigga been staying because he hasn't been staying at the hotel…"

*   *   *

- Red -

I had been in the house with Chunky, she had been acting funny lately, every time I tried to touch her she moved my hand, or if I came into the room she was in she hung up her phone. I was watching Chunky sleep when my phone started ringing. It was Bear, he told me he needed some work from my cousin and we started talking. I asked him where he had been? Bear told me he had an apartment. I haven't talked to Bear in almost a week and he sounded different.

MJ hadn't been around a lot lately so I called his phone and told him Bear called, and he needed some work. I told him what Bear needed and he said he was on his way home. MJ came about 30-minutes after I talked to him, he gave me the work to give to Bear and he told me how much money I was supposed to get back. I called Bear and told him how much money he was supposed to have and I told him to meet me downtown at the train station.

I got in the Impala and drove to the train station. I went in the train station and bought a ticket to Ohio. Then I put the work in a locker and grabbed the key. I sat in the train station for about 20-minutes before Bear called saying he was in front of the train station. I walked out front and got in his Range Rover.

Bear instantly handed me a bag full of money, "it's all there," Bear said and pulled off from in front of the train station.

I opened the bag and looked around the money acting like I was counting it. "Drop me off at the train station to that black Impala," said zipping up the book bag. I handed Bear the key, "the work is in this locker, and can I come see your apartment?"

111

"Yeah, you can come now."

"Let me take this money to my cousin, then I'll call you and get the directions," I said getting out the truck and hopping into the Impala. I drove to the house and MJ was gone, so I called his phone and told him I was about to go to Bear's new apartment. He told me to call him once I was pulling up. I sat the money on the dresser and left out the door and called Bear. "So, where do you live?" I asked Bear and he texted me his address. I put the address in my navigation and started driving toward Bear's apartment.

I pulled up at Bear's apartment and it looked nice. It was a two-flat building, I parked the Impala and got out in my Prada dress and Prada sandals. I called Bear and told him I was outside. Bear came down and opened the door. While I walking up the stairs to Bear's apartment he was behind me and he was putting his hand under my dress rubbing my ass.

"I see you don't have on any panties," Bear said laughing as I slapped his hand away.

"Boy stop, I didn't come over here for that," I said as I got inside the apartment. I started looking around and the apartment was really nice. Bear handed me some weed and told me to roll up a blunt. After, I rolled and lit the blunt, Bear came in the front room with a bottle of Remy 1738, he poured me a cup. I ask him why he hasn't been fucking with MJ and he said he had to find his own way, after the second cup of Remy I was starting to feel the drink and before I knew what was happening Bear was rubbing on my pussy.

I was trying to push his hand away, then he went down and started kissing on my thighs, close to my pussy. I was trying to push Bear's head away but I didn't have any panties on and he was burying his head in my pussy. Before I knew what I was doing, my legs were wide open by themselves. Bear was sucking on my pearl tongue and I was holding the back of his head and grinding my pussy against Bear's face. I felt it coming so I grabbed his head and started grinding harder and I started cumming and squirting everywhere.

I grabbed the back of his head and started moving my hips up and down when my phone started ringing, I reached over on the table and grabbed my phone and it was MJ telling me he needed me to come to the house ASAP. After, hanging up the phone I stood up and told Bear that I had to leave

"Red don't leave me like this," Bear said rubbing on his dick.

"Look Bear I have to go," I said straightening out my dress. Bear had cum all over his face and my dress was sticking to me from cum being all over me.

I left Bear's house and drove straight home. When I got to the house, MJ was sitting in the front room looking out the window.

"Where's Chunky?" MJ asked as soon as I walked through the door.

"When I left she was in the bed sleep."

"And where did you put the money?"

"It's in the room on the dresser," I said walking toward the room.

"Chunky and the money are gone, so don't even bother looking," MJ said never taking his attention from the front room window.

Chapter (21)
- MJ -

I had been at the building with Pablo most of the week, he was really putting the building together, the floors were put in, the whole plumbing and electric system, and most of the drywall. We had the stoves, lights, and paint. I was walking around the building when Red called and said she had taken the money to the house and now she was going to see where Bear lived. So, I finished talking to Pablo and I told Pablo I'll be back and I went to the house.

Once I walked in, I knew something was wrong because it was too quiet. I walked around the house but I couldn't find Chunky. I instantly started looking for the money and when I couldn't find the money I called Red and told her to come home ASAP. I called Chunky's phone five times but no answer. I was in the front room looking out the window when Red walked through the door. After, she explains what she did with the money I knew Chunky had took the money, and the first person I called was Tony.

Tony answered the phone after three rings laughing. "Look Tony, when I had something that belong to you I made sure you got it, now you have something that belong to me, so can I have my money?"

"Look, I am recovering from being shot, plus, I am getting my dick sucked now, so no," Tony said laughing and hung up the phone. I knew right then that I had to get in the field to kill Tony and Chunky, and I was going to need to more than ever.

I walked in the room and Red was sitting on the bed. "So, y'all hoes played me out my money?" I asked walking toward Red.

"MJ, I wouldn't take nothing from you and you should know that."

"Chunky said the same thing.

"I am not that bitch, here I am running around sucking Bear's dick because of you, because you said keep him close. MJ, don't you know I'll do anything for you?"

"Red baby be careful what you say because you're going to have to prove that to me because the punishment for disloyalty is death Red. Now, if this is something you think you can't accept now is the time to get out."

"MJ, I don't want to get out because I am in all the way," Red said looking me in the eyes.

"Red, I'm not going to bull shit you ever. Shit going to get ugly, but I need to know no matter what you're not going to fold on me. I need to trust you with my life because one day my life might depend on you, and yours on me."

"MJ I would do a hundred years in jail before I roll over on you, and I would die before I let something happen to you," Red said with tears coming down her face.

"Red it's me and you, so if you really feel this way about me prove it, show me I am more important to you than anybody else in this world." I told her wiping the tears from her face. I then told Red to roll up a blunt and I went in the front room and started looking out the window, I started thinking that I needed Red and I needed to know if I could trust her.

I walked in the spare room and took out 4 bricks and one of Pop's .380's and sat it on the kitchen counter. Red walked back in the room lighting the blunt, "look, always keep this .380 on you, and this work is going to be in the cabinet. You're going to have to help me find Chunky because y'all grew up together."

"MJ, I'm going to prove to you that I am down with you, just give me a chance."

"Okay, you got it," I said reaching for the blunt. "Come on, let's take a ride." I told Red walking toward the door.

Red drove and we went out south where Chunky's mother lived. She pulled down the block from Chunky's moms house and pulled over.

"This is where my mother stays."

"Let's go meet your mom," I said getting out of the van. Red mother stayed in a two flat building that looked like it had better times.

"Come on, let's go in. But I don't know if she's here." Red got out of the van and as we were walking up to the building I could see someone had the window open with a fan inside the window. We walked up to the door and Red twisted the nob and walked right inside the house and I was right behind her.

When I got inside the house it was cleaner than I thought. Red's mother was sitting on the couch and when she saw us walk through the door she stood up to give Red a hug. Red's mother had on a tank top with no bra, and a pair of thin cotton shorts that might as well have been panties. But Red's mother was pretty as hell, she had gray eyes and looked like she was around 40 years old, yet her body was still looking good.

After, hugging Red she came to me and gave me a hug. I could tell she was a free spirit.

"You know your cousin Evon came up here from New Orleans to see you and you haven't even been home," her mother said calling her cousin Evon from upstairs. Evon came downstairs and surprised the shit out of me. Evon was creole. She had long curly hair with green eyes and her body was well put together. Once Evon seen Red she ran and started hugging her, Evon had a skirt on that was so tight that it looked like it was painted on, with some sandals.

"Girl you had me come up here and you don't even be at home," Evon was telling Red while looking at me. "Girl, where are you about to go because I want to go," Evon said and Red turned to looked at me and I hunched my shoulders.

"Girl hurry up and grab some of your things, I'll be outside," Red said hugging her mother and walking toward the door.

We got in the van and I instantly turned to Red, "that's your family so you better make sure she is under control."

"Look, I already told you you're family, you're my everything and I'll kill that bitch before I let her do or take anything from you."

"That's my bitch, now come here and give daddy a kiss," I said tapping my cheeks.

"Plus, I know you want to fuck her." "How you know I want to fuck her?" I asked Red.

"Because she bad as hell and I want to fuck her," Red said laughing while popping the lock so Evon could get in the van.

Evon came out with a bookbag, she was looking around until Red hit the horn. Evon got in the van talking about how she had been in the house with them old people for weeks, and wanted to have some fun. Red asked me what I wanted to do, and I told her to do her because she was driving. So, she drove out west to where they be selling ecstasy pills, Red give some nigga $60 for 3 flats, and then she drove down the street to the liquor store.

Red went into the liquor store and I told her to get a gallon of Patron and two packs of black jacks. While Red was in the store I turned around and started talking to Evon. "How old are you?"

"I am 23."

"What your nigga says about you coming up here by yourself?"

"I don't have a nigga."

"Are you looking for one?"

"Why, do you know one?" Evon asked looking at me smiling as Red got back in the van.

"Yeah, I know one and when he tries to holla at you don't be acting funny with him either."

"I'm not going to be acting funny," Evon said.

"Where to now?" Red asked getting back in the driver's seat.

"I don't care what you do, you're driving."

"To tell the truth, I want to go in the house," Red said driving toward the house. We pulled up at the house and I could see Evon's eyes open in amazement.

"Girl, I see why you haven't been coming home."

We got out of the van and Andre jumped in as we kept walking to the elevator. Evon had the bag with the drinks inside while Red pushed P for Penthouse. Once the doors opened, Evon started looking around like she was on mars. As soon as Evon sat the bags down Red passed everybody an ecstasy pill and watched us swallow it.

"Girl, I haven't popped a pill in almost 5 years."

"Well, it's on now," Red said pouring me a drink and passing me the cup. "Evon, come in the room with me I'm about to get in the shower."

When Red and Evon went into the other room I jumped in the shower. Once I got out of the shower I put on some gym shorts and a tank top, then went into the other room. Evon was sitting on the bed and Red was in the shower. I grabbed the weed and started rolling up a blunt, "I thought you were getting in the shower?"

"I am, I was letting Red get in first."

"Let me find out you're shy," I said laughing.

"Boy, nobody shy," Evon said hitting her drink. While we were talking Red came out of the bathroom with a towel wrapped around her dreads and tank top on.

"There's a tank top on the hook in there," Red said reaching for the blunt I had in my hand.

"I don't know if it's the hot water or what, but I can already feel that pill, my feet starting to tingling," I said to Red as I passed her the blunt. We had smoked the whole blunt and rolled up another one, I was on my second cup of Patron when I noticed Evon hadn't come out of the

117

bathroom. So, I walked in the bathroom and she was sitting on the floor throwing up. "Evon, are you okay?"

"Yeah, I am feeling a little better since I threw up, but I am rolling hard as hell," Evon said standing up and walking out of the bathroom naked. I grabbed the tank top and walked in the room and passed it to Red.

"Put this on her for me," I said grabbing my drink. Now, I was starting to feel like I was about to throw up from the pill. After, rolling up another blunt and having another drink I was starting to feel better. Red had gone and got Evon some water and they were sitting on the bed talking, I had a California king size bed so all three of us were in the bed with plenty of room.

Red was sitting across from me Indian style, I was looking at Red's pussy and my dick started getting hard. Red was watching me and started smiling, and then started crawling towards me. She pulled my boxers down and started sucking my dick, I could tell Evon was surprised because she was staring at Red while she was sucking my dick. It was feeling so good I couldn't move, I started rubbing my hand through Red's dreads. Red grabbed Evon's hand and pulled her over to where she was. Evon got on her knees between my legs and started sucking my dick too.

I wrapped her long hair in my hand and started guiding her head up and down. I had my eyes closed and my head back when Evon stopped sucking. She just had her mouth open letting me guide her head up and down. I opened my eyes and lifted my head up and instantly saw what was going on, Red was behind Evon eating her pussy from the back. I stood up and got behind Red and started sucking her pussy from the back while she was on her knees eating Evon's pussy.

Then, Red started rubbing and smacking on her own pussy, I stood up and put the head of my dick in Red's pussy and just stood there not moving. Red started pushing back against me harder and harder. I spread Red's ass cheeks and went as deep as I could go and she turned around and looked at me, then I started pounding her out. I pulled out and slapped Red on the ass. "Evon, come here."

Evon took Red's place and put her ass in the air, when I put my dick into Evon she went crazy. She started pulling on the bed sheets, shaking her head from side to side. "Red, get in front of her and open your legs," I said putting as much dick in her as I could. Red was grabbing her hair pulling Evon's head down and making her eat her pussy. Evon started screaming, she was about to cum so I put my thumb in Evon's ass while I started fucking her harder and harder, and then Evon jumped up, turned around, and started looking at me.

Red turned around on her knees and started pushing her ass back against me. I put my thumb in her ass and fucked her 30-minutes straight from the back into I felt myself about to nut, then I grabbed Red by her dreads and made her drink every drop of nut.

Finally, I grabbed some weed and went in the front room and sat in my chair by the window, and started thinking about Chunky and my money.

Chapter (22)
- Bear -

After Red left, I jumped in the shower because I had cum all over my face. When I got out of the shower I went straight to work, I started cooking up the brick of cocaine. Out of the 36 ounces I cooked up 46, plus, I put a little ammonia in it.

Then, I started bagging up the heroin, I took 200 grams and bagged up $25,000 in $50 bags. I called Gunner and asked him how much was he paying for the ounce of cocaine he was getting, when he told me $1250, I told him I had some butter for $1100. He told me to bring him three. I told Gunner that I would be on the block in 30-minutes.

I was leaving the house when Kesha and her brother were on the porch smoking a blunt. When Kesha saw me, she gave me a hug and introduced me to her brother, Money. He was a big nigga with long ass matted dreads, and he had a strong Jamaican accent

"So, you Bear the one my sister keeps talking about?" Money asked me passing me the blunt. I could tell Kesha's brother was getting money, he had diamonds and gold everywhere. We talked on the porch for a minute before Money asked me to go out to eat with them. I told them let me make a run really quick and I'll be back in 20-minutes, then I'll go.

When I pulled up on the block it was looking like someone was having a block party. Fat Mac had bought a yellow 1996 Impala with blue leather insides, and 22-inch rims. Slim had bought a 2017 7-45 BMW; everybody was getting money. As I pulled up Gunner was pulling up in a 2010 Honda, "nigga why you not spending some of that money you got?" I asked Gunner as soon as he got out the car.

"I am spending some of this money, you see I bought a car," Gunner said opening his arms toward the car. I followed Gunner to his mom's house and he gave me a book bag with $17,300 in it and said $3,300 was for the cocaine. I gave him the work and went around the corner to the house, Kesha was on the porch when I pulled up.

"Let me run upstairs real quick," I said getting out the truck and taking the bookbag in the house. When I came back down Kesha and her brother, along with another female who was Money's girl, was waiting on the porch. She was so thick she was almost fat, and her dress was so tight that if she moved the wrong way it looked like it would rip.

"Look, we can all ride in the same car," Money said walking down the stairs toward his car. Money had an all-white 2020 Bentley truck.

"Where are we going?" I asked Kesha on our way to the Bentley truck.

"We're going to a family barbecue," Kesha said getting in the truck. We went somewhere out south, when we pulled up Jamaicans were everywhere. I went with Money and he introduced me to some of his family and I could tell instantly these niggas were getting some real money.

Kesha walked up and I whispered in her ear, "why didn't you tell me your brother was the King around her?"

"Boy, he not no king, but he not no foot soldier either. Why does it matter?" Kesha asked looking at me.

"It doesn't, just asking," I said. Then, Money came over and told me to walk with him. When we got by ourselves, Money turned to me and said he knew I was getting money on Dover. I was surprised I didn't know what to say.

"Look, I'm not knocking your hustle, I'm trying to help you eat while helping me eat at the same time."

"How do you know I am getting money over there?"

"Because I know everything that goes on in my hood. Plus, do you think you're going to be doing almost $30,000 and nobody is going to notice?"

"So, Money what are you talking about?"

"Look, the niggas that was working that block before you, we were at war with them. So, when you popped up we had our antennas up, but this is what I'm going to do. You join the crew. We're going to put some of my niggas on Dover to help your shorties out. You get your work from me and you have access to the block I control. In return, I got Fridays on whatever block you decide to work on."

"What do you mean you got Fridays?"

"I mean I am putting my work on your block on Fridays."

"So, I'm losing out because Fridays' are my best days."

"Naw, you not losing out, because you have more than one block, and now you have an army."

"Fuck it, I'm down,"

121

"That's good and I forgot to say, I am the only person selling weed," Money said laughing. I knew shit was about to get crazy.

After we had our talk, Money took me in the house where there were around 30 niggas smoking and drinking. I told them I was one of the new niggas on the team and surprisingly, they welcomed me with open arms. One of the Jamaicans pointed to the table and told me to roll up a blunt, and when I went to the table there was around 2 pounds just lying there. I rolled a blunt and someone handed me a pint of Remy, and I noticed everybody had their own pint and their own blunt.

After about an hour of smoking and drinking, Money and I went back out to the barbecue. There was a crowd of females dancing and Money turned to me and asked me which one of them I wanted?

"Money, I am kind of fucking with your sister."

"Having one female is too close to zero for me," Money said walking off. I was feeling the Remy so I went and sat down at one of the tables. Kesha came over and started dancing on me while I was sitting down. I was looking around and more and more niggas was showing up.

"Kesha, I'm ready to go to the house."

"Let me get you something to eat first," Kesha said walking off.

I need to talk to Gunner. I don't know nothing about these niggas, but this sound like a good deal because we could both make some money. Yet, if his prices aren't better than Red's cousins then I was going to be on the losing end, I was thinking when Money came over to the table I was sitting at.

"Kesha said you are ready to go, but tonight we're all going to the strip club."

"I can't go because I left some things on the block unfinished."

"Okay. Well, I'll take you back when you're ready," Money said walking off. Kesha came back with two plates of jerk chicken, and jerk steak with cabbage.

After, I got done eating, Kesha went and got Money, and Money and one of his niggas drove me home. While Money was driving I asked him what other blocks they have? Money took me to a block close to where I was already working on Dover. It was around 30 blocks away and when we pulled up wasn't nobody selling anything. "Why isn't anybody working?" I asked Money.

"Because most Jamaicans only sell weight, but that's where you come in at."

"So where are your guys?" I asked Money looking around.

"They're around. Don't worry, when you're ready they'll be here," Money said pulling off and taking me to the house. Once Money pulled up in front of the house, I was walking up the stairs deep in thought. Now I knew Money needed me, but what I didn't know was how much he needed me? When I got in the house I called Gunner and asked where he was, he said he was on the block. I told him I was pulling up and that I needed to talk to him. I jumped in the truck and pulled on the block and Gunner jumped in the truck with me.

"What's going on Big Homie?"

"Well, look, what do you know about the Jamaican nigga name Money?"

"I know he's not to be fucked with and he runs most of the blocks around here, why?"

"Well, I just teamed up with Money, we could work any block and as many blocks as we want, but he just got Fridays," I said looking at Gunner to watch his reaction.

"Look Bear, when you first came around here I said I was fucking with you, so I am fucking with you. Are you asking me if I think that's a good deal? Well, yes and no. Are we going to get rich? Yes, but we are going to war also," Gunner said. As I was listening to Gunner, I seen a boxed Chevy with three niggas watching us but I brushed it off.

Chapter (23)
- MJ -

I had been in my chair thinking and the next thing I knew I was waking up to sunlight coming through the window. I heard some noise to the left of me and when I turned and looked, Evon was going in the refrigerator. "Evon come here," I said standing up with my dick on hard still feeling the pill from last night.

Evon walked over to me naked. I told her to bend over the couch with her ass facing me and to reach her arms behind her and to spread her ass cheeks. I spit on my hand and rubbed Evon's pussy, but it was already dripping wet. I put the head of my dick inside Evon and she started moaning and moving her head from side to side, so I pushed a little further inside her and she let go of one of her cheeks and grabbed her hair and I instantly stop moving.

"Did I tell you to let go? Now spread them," I said slapping Evon hard on her ass. She reached back and spread her ass cheeks. I fucked Evon slow for the first 15-minutes until I see her starting to shake and cum.

Then, I long stroked her for the next 30-minutes. When I was about to nut, I pulled out and nutted all over Evon's back and she crumbled on the couch and didn't move. I walked to the bathroom and got in the shower, and when I got out Red was awake sitting on the bed. "Red, I need you to go to the hospital and check on my brother, and make sure you take the gun I gave you. Call once you get there.

"What about Evon?"

"It's up to you, whatever you do is cool," I said walking to the closet to get dress.

"MJ can I get some money? I need to get some things. Plus, I wanted to take Evon shopping."

"Yeah, I got you, but know your job is to look for Chunky or Tony," I said as Red walked in the bathroom to jump in the shower. I went into the safe in the guest room and took out $5000 and gave it to Red.

Then, I grabbed my bullet proof vest and my gun, and was walking toward the door. When I saw Evon on the couch sleeping, I slapped her ass as hard as I could and Evon jumped up. "Go in there and get your ass in the shower," I said watching Evon get up naked walking in the room without saying anything. I left out the door.

I drove straight to the building Pablo was fixing up and it looked good, the first floor was almost finished, and the only thing that was left to do was paint. I spent the next hour going over things with Pablo, telling him to have everybody focus on the first floor. While we were talking, Old School from the barber shop called saying he needed to see me asap. So, I jumped in the van and drove over to the barber shop. When I walked in, Old School had a bloody towel up against his head

"Old School what happened to you?" I asked Old School looking around the barber shop.

"Some niggas came in here and robbed me, they took everything," Old School said sitting down in one of the barber chairs. So Old School went on to tell me three niggas came in the shop like they were going to get haircuts and upped a gun.

Then, Old School showed me the video tape from the camera and I was surprised to see three Jamaicans coming into the shop and robbing him. But on the video, I saw a black Dodge Charger with a big dent in the back door that the three Jamaicans got out of. Old School was saying how he was going to pay me back when I heard the shots and the barber shop's windows exploded. I was pushed back up against the wall and everything went black.

*   *   *

- Red -

MJ gave me $5000 and I went to jump in the shower. While I was in the shower, Evon came in and looked at me and instantly said MJ told me to come get in the shower. After we both got out of the shower and got dressed, we went downstairs to the car and the first place I went was to the tattoo shop. I got M on one ass cheek real big, and J on the other same size in blue ink. I was already a Redbone so the blue MJ stood out.

After, I was finished, Evon looked at me and said I was crazy but it looked good. From there we went to the Prada outlet in the mall and I got a pair of white Prada stretch pants, a white Prada tank top, and I brought Evon a Prada summer dress and both of us some Prada flip flops.

125

The bill at the Prada store was $900, then we went to the Gucci store and bought a Gucci dress and some Gucci sandals for $1300.

"Is that your car?" Evon asked out of the blue.

"Girl why?"

"And where did you get all that money from?" Evon asked as we went into Footlocker.

"Evon please, don't start asking me all these fucking questions," I said picking up an Ace bandage. Also, I bought MJ two jogging suits and two pair of Air Maxes.

"Are we going back over to MJ's house?" Evon asked me looking down.

"Do you want to go back over MJ's house?" I asked already knowing the answer.

"I don't really care," Evon said trying to sound convincing.

"Well, fuck, we'll go back to mom's house," I said looking at Evon.

"Naw, I didn't say that. I just said I don't care."

"Bitch stop playing with me, you know you want some more of that dick, now don't you?" I said and stared at Evon in her eyes.

"Girl that's your nigga."

"And he still going to be my nigga after y'all fuck. Bitch I don't care so don't think you're being sneaky," I said as we walked out of the store and went to the car.

I drove to the hospital and Evon was quiet the whole ride, as we pulled up in the parking lot I went in my purse and grabbed a blunt and some weed. "Here, roll this up." I told Evon turning the car off. Evon rolled the weed up and we smoked while I called MJ to tell him I was going inside the hospital; but nobody answered the phone. To keep the car safe, I put our bags from shopping inside the truck and went inside the hospital to Demar's room.

While we were walking, there was three niggas with long dreads walking a couple of steps in front of us, but one kept turning around flirting with Evon. She pulled out her phone and started putting his number in her phone.

Then, the other two slowed down and started looking around and called a nurse over, but Evon and I kept walking. As we made it to Demar's room and opened the door, I heard the nurse asking, "where are those young ladies right there going?" Once I heard the nurse say that, I stopped and looked at the three niggas. They looked at each other, turned around and walked away. I continued to walk into the room and instantly called MJ once inside, but once again, no answer. I really needed to tell MJ the Jamaicans were at the hospital.

*   *   *

- MJ -

As I came to I realized that I had been shot twice in the chest, it was hard for me to breathe and I put my hand over my vest where the pain was, but there wasn't any blood.

Then, I realized that I couldn't breathe because the wind had been knocked out of me. When I got my bearings back, I looked around and Old School was hiding behind one of the barber chairs. I stood up and instantly called Gimmy That and told him to come to the barber shop. I saw that I missed two calls on my phone from Red, so I called her back and when she told me the Jamaicans were at the hospital everything made sense. Chunky had told Tony everything.

I was pacing back and forth in the barber shop floor when Gimmy That pulled up. Before anybody in his truck could get out I told them to follow me and I drove to the hospital. Tay Boogie and I went upstairs to Demar's room while Gimmy That and Gotti stayed downstairs in the lobby on point looking for anything out of the ordinary. When I walked through the door of Demar's room Red had her hand in her purse pointing it at me. "What were you about to do with that?" I asked laughing knowing she had the gun in her hand.

"Whatever I had to do," she said looking for real. I told them to stay there while I went to talk to the doctor alone. I explained to the doctor that I wanted to move Demar to his private home to be looked after by a private nurse. The doctor said he didn't agree but since I was his only family it was up to me. I asked the doctor if he could have an ambulance take Demar to his home and the doctor agreed and set everything into motion.

I went back to the room and told Tay Boogie to drive the Impala. And told Gimmy That and Gotti to drive their truck, and Red was going to drive the van. At every light one of the cars was going to stop in the middle of the street and stop traffic so nobody could follow the ambulance, and then the next couple of lights the same thing. As we were talking the doctor and some nurse came in and started prepping Demar to leave. I told Tay Boogie to go tell Gimmy That what to do and I told Red I was riding in the ambulance and five minutes later we were on our way downtown to the condo. Everything went as planned, I had the ambulance driver put Demar in the extra room, and the doctor sent a monitor to watch Demar's vital signs. Once the ambulance drivers had hooked Demar up to the monitor and left, I called Red and told her to come pick me up at the house. I called Tay Boogie and told everybody to meet at Homerun Inn Pizza. It was time to put a plan together.

Chapter (24)
- Bear -

After I talked to Gunner I went to the house and bagged up 200 grams in all $50 bags. I had bagged up $39,000. I knew Kesha and Money were still at the barbecue so I called Kesha and told her to bring me some of that jerk chicken. Then I called Money and told him I was going to start working on the block he showed me when he dropped me off. Money said go ahead and he was going to have some of his niggas to be on both blocks tomorrow. So, after I got the okay from Money, I called Gunner and explained to him what was going on and that we were opening up shop on the new block at 6:00 in the morning. After I put the work up I got in the shower and put on a tank top and some boxers, then rolled me two blunts and grabbed a pint of Remy out of the refrigerator.

I sat on the couch smoking and drinking thinking about New York. I was thinking that I needed to get Tom-Tom up here to watch my back. After drinking the whole pint, I must have nodded off because the next thing I knew my phone was ringing and someone was knocking on my door at the same time. When I went to answered the door, Kesha and some females were standing there, so I left the door open and went and sat back down on the couch. Kesha walked in carrying a plate of food, I grabbed my phone and looked at the time and it was 4:00 in the morning.

"Bear, this is my brother's bm Tiffany." Kesha must have seen me looking at the time on my phone because she said Money and his niggas went to the strip club and now my momma locked the door. Kesha and Tiffany both were drunk as hell. I was watching Tiffany, she was black as hell, but pretty. She was about 5'6 and around 120 pounds, and had long red dreads. Tiffany was skinny, but something about her told me she was freaky. I could see it in her eyes. Kesha and Tiffany both had on skirts with heels on. I was on one couch and Tiffany and Kesha was on the other couch together and they both was falling asleep. So, I tapped Tiffany and told her she could get on the couch I was on before I went in my room and got in the bed. Only then did I realize that Tiffany was the female in the car with Money.

I was thinking about that when Kesha came into my room, she instantly grabbed my boxers and pulled them down and started sucking my dick. Kesha had put my dick in her throat and started moving her head up and down while slurping at the same time, and before I knew it I was nutting down Kesha's throat. I couldn't do anything but be still like a baby, and Kesha rolled over and went to sleep. I was laying there but I knew I had to open up the block at 6:00am and that was in like another hour.

So, I got up and went in the front room to get my weed. I sat on the couch and started rolling up a blunt when I looked over at Tiffany, her dress had raised up and her pussy was showing. Tiffany didn't have on any panties, so I was getting a good look, but I knew that Tiffany was Money's baby momma. Instead, I grabbed a lighter off the table and lit the blunt and turned my attention to watching the TV. Tiffany must have smelled the weed because she opened her eyes and saw me smoking weed and looking her way.

Then, Tiffany noticed that her dress was raised up and I was looking at her pussy. All of a sudden Tiffany did something that blew my mind. While I was looking at her, she opened her legs and started playing with her pussy, then she took her fingers out her pussy and started sucking on them. I couldn't help myself and I found myself walking over to the couch where Tiffany was and started rubbing on her pussy. I pulled down my boxers and she started spreading her legs open farther and farther.

As soon as I put my dick in her I knew I was in trouble. Tiffany grabbed my ass and started pulling me deeper and deeper inside her while she was grinding her hips, and trying to pull me in deeper. She pushed me off of her and got on top of me and started riding, I had my eyes closed, but I felt myself about to nut so I started trying to push Tiffany off of me, but she started moving her hips faster and faster.

"Tiffany! I'm about to nut," I said grabbing her hips trying to push her off of me. She started grinding her hips faster and faster, and then I started nutting and she started cumming at the same time as she collapsed on my chest. "Tiffany you know I nutted in you," I said trying to get up before Kesha came out of the room.

"Boy I heard you the first time you said it, and nobody going to get pregnant," Tiffany said sitting up finally letting me get up. I went back to the other couch and picked up the blunt I dropped off the floor and lit it right up.

I grabbed my phone and looked at the time and it was 5:30am. "Look I got to go, I'll be back later on today," I said looking at Tiffany.

"Boy I have to go too, Money will kill me if he knew I was over here. Can I get in your shower really quick?"

"Yeah, go ahead," I said going in the room with Kesha as Tiffany got in the shower just in case Kesha woke up. It only took Tiffany five minutes to get in and out of the shower. I made my way back in the front room once I heard her in there.

"Well, I'm about to go," Tiffany said walking towards the door.

I walked up to Tiffany and put my hand under her dress and put two fingers inside her pussy, "don't go home with that pussy smelling like soap," I said taking my fingers out of her and opening the door.

"Yeah, you right Tiffany," said leaving.

I instantly went in the room and woke up Kesha, "I'm about to go."

"Well, can I stay here for a little while because it's too early for me to go home?" Kesha asked turning her face to me.

"Look Kesha, I am not going to trip, but if my bitch comes over just let her in," I said seeing what Kesha would say. She just said okay and turned around and went back to sleep. So, I grabbed the work and was out the door.

First, I called Gunner and he said he was walking out the door. I told him to wait in the hallway of his building because I was pulling up. Gunner already told me Slim was on the other block with ten of the shorties that was on Dover. Fat Mac should be on Dover with the other ten shorties I was thinking when I pulled up and Gunner was standing in the hallway of his building. I got out the truck and gave Gunner $30,000 worth of $50 bags and I took the other $9,000 to Slim on the other block.

When I pulled up on the new block where Slim was, there was around twenty-five customers waiting on free bags. I pulled up and told Slim to tell the customers we were doing the pass out in ten minutes.

Next, we set up security. I told two people to go to the beginning of the block and I wanted two niggas on the end of the block all looking out for police.

Then, I put one shorty in the south alley and one in the north alley, so the police can't come through. The other four shorties are working the pack and watching the customers, and every hour everyone switch positions. I gave Slim the work and told him to pass out $2,000 worth and everything else gets sold.

131

It was six bags in a pack, the workers get $50 and turn $250 back to Slim. I was riding around picking up customers and dropping them off on the block, by 11:00 am we had done $1250, so I called Money and asked him where was his niggas that said they was coming on the block and he said that they would be here in thirty-minutes.

Money pulled up with ten more niggas and sent those ten niggas on Dover from the ten niggas being on the new block. Traffic started picking up from customers seeing all the people standing out and more and more customers started pulling over and shopping. We were posted on the block about twenty-five deep. Money and his crew had cups of Remy, "where the rest of the drink? I asked Money looking around for the bottle.

"There's some in my car," Money said pointing to his car down the block. So, I walked to the car and I was surprised to see Tiffany in the car.

"Where the drink?" I asked Tiffany looking down at Money.

"It's right here," Tiffany said opening her legs and showing me her pussy.

"Girl pass me the drink," I said laughing and looking around the car. Tiffany passed me the drink laughing also. I went back to where Money was standing and the whole time I was thinking about Tiffany.

I was watching traffic when I saw this same blue Chevy come around with three niggas inside at the stop sign not moving, just looking our way. When they notice I was paying attention they pulled off. I instantly called Gunner and told him to watch out for the blue Chevy while he was out here watching the block.

Money had been on the block for almost two hours and he said he was about to go. I stayed on the block about an hour after Money left. I grabbed the money from Slim we had $3,500. When I made it home Kesha was gone, as I sat down on the couch Gunner called and said he needed four ounces of cocaine. So, I grabbed the work and shot back out the door. Customers were everywhere when I made it back to the block. I parked around ten cars down and I that's when I see the blue Chevy again. Gunner came and got in the car with me and gave me $18,400. Most of it was from the block. I handed Gunner the four ounces, and then I asked Gunner did he know the niggas in the blue Chevy that was parked up there?

"That's Tank and his crew. Tank is a stick-up man, but his bitch stays in the building he was parked in front of. He always parked there," Gunner said getting out of the car.

I went to the house making sure I wasn't being followed and once I made it there, I made a mental note to get rid of Tank and his whole crew.

Chapter (25)
- MJ -

We all met at Homerun Inn Pizza - me, Red, Evon, Gotti, Gimmy That, and Tay Boogie.

"What's going on?" Tay Boogie asked looking around.

"Look, we have to hit them niggas now, no more waiting. We're going to start from the bottom if we have to, so we're in the club every night and in the day time we're on the block. We have to find some of these niggas."

"Well, I have one of them niggas' numbers that was at the hospital," Evon said pulling out her phone.

"Evon, call that nigga and see what's up with him and where is he at. See if he's trying to go out on a date with you, but don't sound to thirsty," I said.

Evon called the nigga, "he said he was out south but he wasn't on shit. He supposed to be on his way to Homerun Inn to pick me up," Evon finished. She told him she was at a birthday party with her family, she asked the nigga who name was C-Murder what kind of car was he riding in? He instantly said an Audi A8 all white. So, I told them I'll be right back. I rode to the gas station and bought a gas can, funnel, two packs of blunts, and $5 worth of gas.

I filled the gas can up and rode through the blocks into I found an abandoned building, which didn't take that long. Then I went back to the restaurant. Gotti and I went and got the van while Tay Boogie and Gimmy That went and got in the truck. Red and Evon stayed in the restaurant and waited on C-Murder to call. I told Evon and Red how to play everything. I told Red to call my phone and leave her phone on so I could hear everything. I heard Evon's phone ringing and she said something, then Red said, "he'll be here in five minutes."

Five minutes later, a white Audi pulled up and Red and Evon came out the restaurant. C-murder was in the car by himself and he'd parked right in front of the restaurant. I could hear everything over Red's phone. Evon asked C-Murder could he drop Red off because her guy stood her up? C-Murder said sure, then Red and Evon got in the car with Red getting in the back seat. Before C-Murder could put the car in drive

Red slapped C-Murder in the head with the .380 and told him not to move.

Gotti got out the truck and went to the front driver side's door of the Audi and told C-Murder to move over. Evon got out the Audi and got in the truck with Gimmy That, soon as Evon got in the truck I pulled off. Gotti pulled off right behind me and Gimmy That pulled behind him, my phone was still on speaker and I could her C-Murder saying he didn't have any money. I pulled the van in the alley behind the abandoned building and I grabbed the gas can and the rest of the things I got from the gas station. I also grabbed some duct tape out the van.

Gotti got C-Murder out the car and Red got out with her guns still pointed at C-Murder. Gimmy That parked his truck as Tay Boogie parked my van and everybody came in the abandoned building, Gotti taped C-Murder hands and feet together.

"Look, I am going to ask you one time, where's Tony?" I asked C-Murder taking a blunt out and rolling up some weed.

"I don't know who you're talking about," C-Murder said looking scared. I grabbed his phone and it was one of them iPhones that needed his fingerprint to unlock it. Once I opened the phone I passed it to Red and told her to take a picture of all his numbers. I went and grabbed a brick off the floor and smashed it against his knee and he started screaming.

"Look C-Murder, I'm going to ask you this one more time, how do I find Tony?"

"I don't know where he lives, but his cousin lives on 75th and King Dr., that's the only thing I know."

"What's his cousin's name?" I demanded.

"His name is Stan, and he drives a black BMW." I grabbed the bag and took the funnel out and shoved it down C-Murder's throat.

Then, I took the gas can and poured gas down the funnel filling up his stomach with gas.

Next, I told Red to light the blunt I rolled and to get a nice cherry on it, after she did that I told her to dump the blunt down the funnel and when she did C-Murder's stomach lit up! C-Murder burned from the inside out, fire came out the nigga's mouth like a dragon. When we left out of the abandoned building, I busted the window of C-Murder's car and poured the gas in there also and lit it on fire. Evon, and Red and I got in the van and we went to the house while Tay Boogie, Gotti, and Gimmy That got in the truck and went out south.

While I was driving home, Red looked at me and said that shit made her pussy wet, and when I looked over at her, she looked different, she looked like she really enjoyed it. As I was driving I was looking through the rear-view mirror and Evon wasn't saying anything, "Evon, are you ready to go back to New Orleans yet? I asked her just to see what she would say.

"Naw, I don't want to leave, I want to stay with y'all."

"Look Evon, this shit is no game," I said looking at her in the rear-view mirror.

"I know this isn't a game, just let me prove myself."

"Evon there are rules to being in this family and the first rule is never talk to the police no matter what. Don't let them trick you by telling you somebody told on you. Just always remember, if the police grab you don't say shit but I want a lawyer. Don't answer no questions, just ask for a lawyer. If you ever get locked up for anything one of us will come bond you out okay?"

"Okay,"

"And Evon, if you ever lie you're gone, no second chances because you don't have to lie to me about shit, do you hear me?"

"Yes!"

We got out of the van and went into the building and I went straight to Demar's room to check on him. Once I saw he was alright, I went to get in the shower because I could smell the gas on me. I got out of the shower and Red got in the shower next, and Evon came and got in the bed with me.

"MJ I'm not scared of nothing."

"Evon, the only thing I ask is not to break any of my rules and don't ever be ashamed to tell me anything." I was telling Evon when Red came out the shower. Evon got up and went into the bathroom as Red came over to where I was sitting on the bed and turned around, I couldn't believe what Red was showing me. She had my name tat-totted all over her whole ass in big blue blocks letters. I grabbed Red and gave her a hug and kissed her on her forehead.

*　　*　　*

- Tony -

I've been trapped in this condo out south with Princess, but she's been trying to get back on my good side by telling me all about MJ's spots, who then turned out to be Demar's brother. Princess told me about a barber shop and I sent my niggas inside and they hit for $110,000 and two bricks of cocaine. I had my nigga hitting all of MJ's spots because my arm was still in a sling from getting shot in the shoulder the night my brother was killed.

Princess had told me about a chain of hotels where MJ was working and one of them he stayed in. But from me showing Princess so much attention my bm was starting to get upset, so they were staying on different floors. I've been staying on 77th and Woods at the two flats building where nobody would ever think to look for me. My shoulder was starting to feel better but I couldn't wait so I sent three niggas to the hospital to get the nigga Demar, but somebody was up there watching that nigga and shit was about to get real.

*　　*　　*

- Princess -

That nigga MJ has been leaving messages on my phone asking me where was I, but I didn't respond and I know that bitch Red has something smart as shit to say. I should text his phone and tell him that now he could have the bitch Red. MJ thought I was about to be sitting around while him and Red were always gone. Then, he stops fucking me and was only fucking Red. Fuck that! I could be with Tony for that. I told Tony where that nigga MJ lives and to make sure he kills that bitch Red.

Chapter (26)
- MJ -

The next morning, I got up at 6:00am and started getting dressed. Red and Evon were still in bed. I grabbed my vest and gun, and was out the door. I drove out south on 75th and King Dr. and parked the van and looked for the black 7-45 that Tony's cousin Stan was supposed to have. It took me about twenty-minutes to find Stan's car, so I parked about five cars down from the black 7-45 and waited. It took three hours before somebody came out and got in the car.

He was a fat short nigga with short wavy hair, from where I was sitting in the van. I could see Stan had a Rolex and it was iced out. I followed Stan as he went to some restaurant and he came out with a coffee and a bag, then he drove on 63rd and Woods. I guess this was a block they were working because there were around fifteen niggas out there at 7:00am, and customers was coming and going. Stan had got out of his car and was sitting on a porch eating whatever was in the bag and drinking his coffee.

After watching Stan for about an hour, somebody walked up and handed him some money. Stan walked to his car and went back and sat on the porch. The block he was working was booming. By 11:00am Stan had gone to his car three times. I watched Stan until 5:00pm when he went back to his house. After Stan went to the house, I went to the surplus store and bought a U.S. mail suit and I went to the post office and bought a priority box before going back to my house.

Once I walked in the house, there was a young white girl who looked to be around twenty-one in the room with Demar. She had on some nurse scrubs, so I knew she was caring for him. When I walked into the room, Demar was naked and the nurse was washing him up. Red came out of the room and was standing outside Demar's room door looking at us, the nurse was 5'5 and weighed about 145 pounds. To be white she had a black girl body, she had light blond hair and bright blue eyes. Red came into the room and introduced us, the nurse was Dana.

I walked out of the room after meeting the nurse and Red followed me saying that Dana used to help her mom out when she hurt her back. She said she hope I didn't mind her calling Dana, but that

Dana works at the hospital. I told Red I didn't care and I was proud of her and started walking toward my room with Red on my heels. Evon was rolling a blunt when I walked in the room. I put the shit I had bought in the closet and then grabbed the blunt from Evon as I went in the front room and sat in my chair. I blazed the blunt as I watched Dana finish cleaning Demar. I called Dana in the front room and asked her how long he was going to be like that? She said she couldn't tell at this point and he could come out of the coma in ten minutes, or ten years. I told her thank you and she went back in the room with Demar as I sat there smoking my blunt thinking about tomorrow.

Dana had grabbed her things out of the room and said she'll be back tomorrow. I finished smoking the blunt and went into the room to take a nap because I had to get up in a couple of hours.

*   *   *

- *Gimmy That* -

Tay Booie, Gotti and I were riding out south and we saw some of Tony's niggas hustling on 79th and Evans.

"Gimmy That, pull through the alley," Tay Boogie said rubbing the Mac-11 that was on his lap. I pulled the truck in the alley and parked as all three of us jumped out.

We went through the gangway and watched the block. It was about seven to eight niggas shooting dice on a porch, exactly across the street from where we were ducking down in the gangway. But it looked like they had security on the porches while the workers were walking up and down the streets.

"On the count of three, we're going to go. Gimmy That, you get the nigga on the porch to the right, and I'll get the other nigga on the porch to the left. Tay Boogie, since you got the Mac, you fuck the dice game up," Gotti said putting his hood on his head.

At the count of three, I ran out first with Gotti coming out next. I had a thirty shot .40 Cal and I shot the nigga on the porch twice in the chest. Gotti shot eight times with the first two shots hitting the other nigga twice in the arm making him drop his gun on the porch. Tay Boogie had sprinted to the crowd that was shooting dice and they didn't stand a chance. The first two he shot head exploded, then they started to run. Tay Boogie shot two more niggas in the back, and then he ran up on the two niggas that was on the ground and gave each one of them a head shot.

Then he turned around and emptied the clip on the crowd of customers that was trying to run. The whole time that Tay Boogie was going crazy with the Mac, Gotti and I were standing in the gangway making sure nobody ran out of the house trying to get a lucky shot. Once Tay Boogie was out of shells we ran back to the truck and slowly pulled out of the alley, but I didn't see the Jamaican that was standing on the side of the garage. He jumped out with two .9 mm pointed at the front window. Tay Boogie was looking down at the Mac-11 when the shots went off.

I ducked under the steering wheel. All I could hear was bullets hitting the window, so I hit the gas and made shorty that was shooting touch every tire on the truck. When I raised up there wasn't anything wrong with the window, Tay Boogie and I looked at each other at the same time as we pulled off.

"Pull up on 47th and Woods," Tay Boogie said.

"Tay Boogie, there's nothing but Jamaicans over there," Gotti said from the back seat.

"I know, but the police not going to be able to be at both places at the same time," Tay Boogie said as he loaded the Mac-11.

I drove though the block and there was a couple of niggas out shooting basketball on a rim in somebody drive way, then there were two niggas hugged up with two females. I dropped Tay Boogie off in front of the block and drove down the block. As soon as I turned I parked, and Gotti and I got out of the truck and went around the corner we started walking up the block.

After around ten feet, I could see Tay Boogie walking on the other side of the street. He was on the side of the street they were playing basketball. Gotti and I were on the other side where the two niggas and their girls were on the porch talking. We walked up to the porch and I asked one of the niggas do they got any weed around here? One of them looked over to the guys that was playing basketball. But before he could call anybody Gotti had taken out his .45 and started shooting at the porch. I turned around and started shooting at the niggas that was playing basketball and they started running towards Tay Boogie trying to get away from the heat I was putting down.

Tay Boogie waited until they were five feet from him, then he upped the Mac-11 and went bananas! A couple of the Jamaicans turned around and started running away from Tay Boogie, but I was right there. One nigga was on the ground from a leg shot and another nigga was running. I ran up and cut him off grabbing him by his shirt and shot him twice in the chest.

Then, I shot the nigga that was laying on the ground in the head. I saw Tay Boogie running my way and I turned around as we ran to the truck leaving seven niggas dead and three more shot.

*   *   *

- MJ -

I got up the next morning at 5:00am thinking about Tony, I grabbed some weed and went in the room with Demar and blazed my blunt thinking about what was about to go on and wishing that Demar was out of his coma.

After, I finished smoking the blunt, I went in the room and woke up Red and Evon and told them to get dressed. I grabbed my bullet proof vest and my .40 Cal with the thirty-shot clip and I put the mailman suit in a bag so nobody would see it in the elevator. Once everybody got dressed and out the door, I told Red to drive and where to go. At 6:00am, we pulled in front of Stan's house. I changed into the mailman suit in the van and waited. While we were waiting I told Red and Evon what I wanted them to do.

Yesterday, Stan came out of the house at 7:00am, so I was expecting him to come out at that same time, but by 8:00am he still haven't come out. I grabbed the priority box I bought the other day and got out of the van and walked up to Stan's door and rang the bell with the priority box in my hand. My gun in the other hand under the box. It took five minutes before Stan came and opened the door. When he did he had a cup in his hand. I passed him the box and once he felt how light it was I spoke, "Stan, please don't make me shoot you, now who all is in this house?" I asked Stan pushing him back inside with the barrel of my gun.

"Please, brother don't shoot, nobody is here but me and my girl," Stan said putting his hands in the air. I waited by the door for about two more minutes before Red and Evon came in with the duct tape.

"Where's the females?" I asked Stan putting my finger to my mouth telling him to be quiet.

141

"She went back in the back room on the left," he said. Red walked off with her .380 in her hand.

Evon duct taped Stan's hands and mouth while I had the gun pointed at him. Red came out with a skinny bitch with long braids and glasses so Evon could duct tape her hand and mouth also.

I turned to Stan. "First, you're going to tell me where's the money and work, or you're going to die," I said looking Stan straight in the eye. Before he could respond I spoke again. "Now, when I take this tape off your mouth. If it's anything but where the money at, I'm going to kill you and search for it myself. And if I don't find it cool." And I took the tape off Stan's mouth.

"Everything inside the stove," Stan said singing like a bird. I nodded to Red and she walked off going into the kitchen.

"And make sure you don't leave any finger prints," I said to Red. "Now Stan, there's one more thing… where's Tony?" I asked and I could tell he was surprised.

"I don't know!" Stan said.

I walked off and went in the kitchen with Red, she was pulling two bookbags out of the oven. I grabbed a knife and told Red to search the rooms good and to make sure to wipe her prints off of anything she touched and I went back in the front room with Stan. I walked right up to him and stabbed him in the leg, "now please stop playing with me, where does Tony live?" I asked again twisting the knife around in my hand.

"He lives on the north side of Kimball and Belmont in a two flat building two houses from the corner."

"I'm about to send someone there now while I wait here and if you're lying you are dead."

"Look, he in a whole building, first and second floor, the building has a red front door," Stan was saying before Red came out the back with another book bag.

"You see Stan, I found some more money which means you're a liar and you might be lying about Tony's whereabouts too."

"Look, I'm telling you the truth about that," Stan said.

I walked over to Evon and handed her the knife and whispered in her ear. Evon didn't hesitate and walked right up to Stan's girl and sliced her throat. Stan started screaming, I nodding at Evon and she walked over and sliced Stan's throat too. Each one of us grabbed a bag and we walked out the house one at a time. We handed to the house to regroup.

Chapter (27)
- Bear -

I had got a call from Money telling me he was on his way to come get me, and twenty-minutes later Money pulled up in a black Dodge Charger. When I got in the car with him he was talking fast on the phone with somebody. All I could hear was somebody screaming and Money saying he was going to look into it. When Money hung up the phone he stared ahead not saying anything. "What's going on?" I asked Money and he just opened up and told me everything.

"All our blocks out south have been getting hit. In the last two days around twelve niggas have been killed. Now we're going out south to check on some of the blocks."

When we made it out south there was only a couple of niggas on the block. When Money asked what happen nobody knew nothing and nobody was selling anything. The more we rode around the south the more I noticed that people were on their porch. Teddy Bears and Balloons were on every other block. You could not only see death, but feel death everywhere out there. Money had got on his phone and called somebody, and as we drove down a couple more blocks Money pulled over and two niggas came out.

One nigga had a sling around his arm and the other nigga had a Mac-11 in his hand. Money asked the nigga with the sling on his arm what happen and he said he didn't know.

"We were playing basketball and two niggas came up shooting. I don't know them and don't know why they was shooting at us."

As he was talking a car sped pass and I could see the fear in the nigga's eyes that was talking.

"We don't know what type of car they was riding in or how the niggas look."

They knew nothing. Money pulled off headed toward the north side, "we have to put extra security on both of our blocks just to make sure we don't get caught slipping."

"Look Money, I'm going to need some work, so what's the price?"

"The heroin books go for $60,000, and I'll give you the cocaine for $27,500."

"Okay, Money. I still got a little work left that I already have, but I am going to need that A.S.A.P."

"Look Bear, I am about to lay low for about a week, just be on point. I'll take you to grab the work now," Money said calling somebody on his phone.

It took us around thirty-minutes and we were pulling in an alley, then going into a garage. Once out the garage we walked in a two flat building and went downstairs into the basement. From the outside of the building looked like it was abandoned, but once inside the building everything was brand new. There was a pool table, video games, a 100-inch TV screen, surround sound, and marble countertops in the kitchen. I was amazed from looking at the outside, and you'll never think the inside looked like this. Not in a million years.

We sat down on the couch and there was a pound of weed on the table. "Rolled up," Money said calling someone on his phone. Twenty-minutes later a big nigga with long dreads came down the stairs carrying a book bag. Money introduced us saying the nigga name was Tony, I didn't know Tony but he looked familiar and I couldn't remember from where. He went into the refrigerator and grabbed a fifth of Patron and we smoked and drank talking about cash.

Tony was telling Money that he shut down all his blocks. He then asked Money if he wanted to work some of them for a couple of months. Money said he didn't know and had to think about that for a minute. Tony excused himself and he went upstairs and came back down with a big bowl of jerk chicken. We smoked, drank, and ate, and then we smoked and played a game. Money said we had to stay there and leave out with morning traffic so it would look like we were going to work because Tony's house might be hot from all the shooting that was going on.

Once it was 5:00am, Money grabbed the bag and we went out to the garage, and soon as we were in the car Money handed me the book bag. We pulled out of the garage and I felt like someone was watching us, but it could have been from Money talking about Tony being hot. I brushed it off and laid my head back in Money's car. Something told me to lift my head up and I saw a van ride past and turn off, and for a second, I thought I saw Red's face in the driver seat, but I brushed it off again.

145

Chapter (28)
- MJ -

I couldn't sleep because I wanted this nigga Tony. I woke up around 3:00am and called Gimmy That, I gave them the directions to Tony's house. I told them to find a park in front of the house and call me when they get there.

After, Red and Evon got up and grabbed everything we needed we were out the door. Before we made it to Tony's house, Tay Boogie called and said they were in front of a house, but didn't know if it was the right house. Red was driving so I told her to park in the back of the house in the alley. While we were parked, I was on the phone with Tay Boogie when the garage door opened and a white Bentley coupe came out. I told Red to pull off behind the car.

When the Bentley pulled out of the alley, Red was fifteen feet behind the Bentley. When the Bentley pulled up to a red light I told Red to pull alongside of it. I looked out the back-side window of the van and noticed the driver, but it wasn't Tony. As the light turned green I told Red to go back to the alley. While she was pulling off from the light I saw Bear, sitting back up in the passenger seat. I couldn't believe my eyes, because all I knew was the driver of the Bentley was a Jamaican.

So, was this nigga Bear fucking with these niggas?

As we were pulling off I never told Red what I saw and we parked back in the back of Tony's house. I started daydreaming... *pops had told me when we first met, to find out what your enemy's most afraid of and you'll always find out what their most eager to believe...* I came out of my day dream and knew what I had to do.

I told Evon and Red the plan. Then I called Tay Boogie and told him what I wanted him to do.

Next, I looked at my phone and it was 5:00am. I told Tay Boogie that we were going to set the plan in motion at 7:00am and I got to work. I got in the back of the van and ripped Evon's shirt and her stretch pants, then I got out the van and grabbed a hand full of dirt and wiped the dirt all over Evon's face and chest.

After that, I hit her twice in the mouth and she got out of the van bleeding, and then walked around to the front of Tony's building. Once

Evon was in the front of Tony's house she called the police and started hollering and screaming for help.

Lastly, Evon gave the police the address to where she was and then she hung up the phone. Twenty minutes later it sounded like the whole police force was coming. The police and ambulance came up the one way with sirens and lights flashing. I waited for about five minutes, then I walked through the gangway three houses down from Tony's. Once I was on Tony's block, I watched the police talking to Evon while the whole neighborhood was on their porch watching. Wondering what was going on and why the police was there. I walked up to Tony's house wearing my mail man suit.

So much shit was going on with Evon and the police no one even noticed me. When I reached Tony's porch I was about to ring the doorbell before I saw some pretty ass female looking out the window. So, I pointed to the package in my hand and waved at her to come downstairs. It took her maybe, three or four minutes before she came downstairs holding her robe together with one hand. Soon as she opened the door I put my gun to her stomach, and pushed her inside the vestibule, then told her that if she said anything she would die, but this had nothing to do with her.

"Who's in the building?" I asked her.

"Tony is upstairs and Princess is downstairs," she said nervously thinking about dying.

We waited in the vestibule for another three minutes before Tay Boogie and Gimmy That came in and joined us. I told them both that Tony was upstairs, and not to kill him as they handed upstairs.

After another three minutes of waiting, Red and Gotti came in. I instructed them two to go on the first floor and get Chunky. "Take her to the basement, but don't hurt her."

I push the other females I was holding toward Red. "Take her too, and she is going to show you how to get down there."

Then I went upstairs. Tay Boogie and Gimmy That had Tony tied up while they were searching the house. Once Tony saw my face he started begging. "Look nigga, I am going to give you one chance to tell me where the money and work is, and I promise you that I won't kill you," I said walking up close to Tony's face.

"I know, you're going to let one of your niggas kill me, right?" he asked showing fear in his eyes.

147

"Look nigga, I am not here to make deals, show me where the shit is and you live. You don't you die!" I said turning around.

"Okay, open the cabinets under the kitchen sink, then push on it and it will pop open," Tony said.

I went in the kitchen and did exactly what Tony said, there was five bricks of heroin with around $300,000. "Take Tony to the basement and then come back to get the money and the work." I told Gimme That.

When I got downstairs I got right to business. Chunky saw me and started crying and saying sorry. I grabbed the bag that I had told Red to bring with her and begin to tape Tony's hand and feet up really good with the duct tape.

Then I pulled out the scissors and the lighter fluid as I slapped him upside his head with my .40 Cal until he was unconscious. "Take the two females in the other room and watch them." I directed Red before I focused on Tony.

Next, I took the scissors out and I cut his tongue out while he was unconscious. After I cut his tongue off, Tony came to and started trying to holler, but no words would come out.

After that, I took the lighter fluid and the scissors. I cut the pupil in both of Tony's eyes out and then sprayed lighting fluid in both of his eyes. I bent down and whispered in Tony's ear. "Always remember, you fuck up because you touched my family."

Continuing, I then took the scissors and stuffed them in his ears busting his ears drums. I begin squirting the lighting fluid in his ears and lit his ass on fire. I let Tony burn for 3 to 4 minutes before I poured some water on him putting the fire out. Tony was on the floor flopping like a fish out of water. As I turned around, Tay Boogie and Gimmy That were looking at me like I was crazy. I walked over to the window and saw the police were gone. Then I went in the room with Red and told her to kill both of them. Red shot the both of them in the head once.

"Come on, grab the money and work and let's go," I said very loud as I walking towards the door.

"What about Tony, you're just going to leave him here alive?" Tay Boogie asked looking at me shocked.

"Who is he going to tell? He ca not talk because I cut his tongue out, he can't see or hear because I burned his eyes and ears. So, he isn't going to tell shit. He's a walking vegetable," I said walking towards the door.

I gave Tay Boogie, Gotti, and Gimmy That the money and I took the work and left out the back door. They went out the front. Once me and Red made it to the van Evon was in the back seat, "Red, drive to the house," I said thinking about Tony.

For as long as Tony lives he's going to know that I did this to him and he's not going to be able to tell anybody. Now it's time to get Bear ass, since he wants to switch sides... I was thinking to myself as Red drove home.

"What happened to Tony?" Evon asked as we drove though the Chicago streets.

"He's fucked up, but he's alive," I told Evon as I sat in the back of the van and returned to my thoughts.

It was time to get rid of Bear. He was fucking with the Jamaicans. Plus, he hasn't called Red back to pay her that money or reup for more work, so he must be getting his work from somebody else. I know I have to look at Bear like a gazelle. Pops said a gazelle goes out and eat grass because it thinks it's feeding itself, but it's not, it's feeding the lion. Fattening itself up to be food. It was born to be prey and that's the gazelle's only purpose in life and I have to look at Bear the same way... I was thinking when Red pulled up at the condo.

Once inside the condo I grabbed me a blunt and went in the room with Demar and was talking to him while he was in a coma. I told him about Tony. How I fucked him up, and then I told him about Bear. I was telling him what Pops had told me always assume your enemies are cleverer than you give them credit for beecause even an animal can think seven steps ahead. So, I was going to spend some time watching Bear before I made my next move, then out of nowhere I heard a weak voice say, "time can be a greedy thing sometime, it stills all the details for itself."

As I looked over it was Demar weakly opening his eyes. I was shocked that I didn't know what to do or say, until Demar told me he needed some water. I went and got Demar some water, and he was so weak that he could not even lift up his hand to grab the cup, but Demar was awake!

To Be Continued....

Acknowledgements

I dedicate this book to my rock, my mother Ms. Davis, who has installed the drive in me to chase my dreams no matter what it is. And the streets of the Westside of Chicago for being an inspiration for my vision. I want to give a shot out to my uncle Anthony Davis -99, keep your head up Unk we're coming for you, and last but not least I want to thank So You Can Write Publications, let's get it.

SO YOU CAN WRITE
PUBLICATIONS®

www.sycwp.com
home4writers@sycwp.com
"Where the writers go…"